Michelangelo

Poems of Love

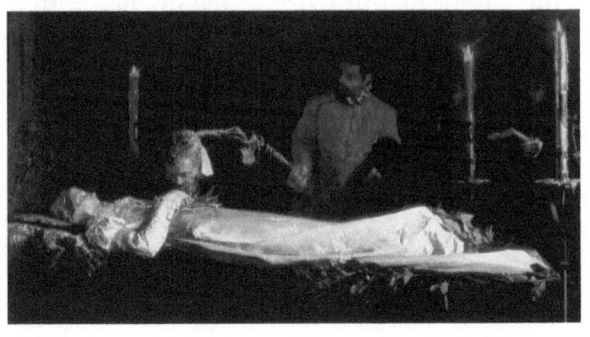

Translated and introduced by

JAMES COWAN

Balgo Hills
Publishing

Copyright © 2021 James Cowan Estate

Written in 2017

All rights reserved.

The author has asserted his right to be identified as the author of this work in accordance with the Copyright, Design and Patents Act 1988.

ISBN-13: 978-1-913816-60-5

First published in this edition: 2021

by Balgo Hills Publishing

Illustration on title page:

Michelangelo beside the body of Vittoria Colonna by Francesco Jacovacci (Italian, 1838–1908)

Cover & Book Design: Amedée & Benjamin

Contents

Introduction   1

Love poems of Michelangelo   95

Appendix   118

INTRODUCTION

1

In the history of western art there are but few titans. Leonardo da Vinci, Rembrandt and Francesco Goya perhaps, certainly Pablo Picasso, and maybe even Auguste Rodin come to mind. The list is not a long one because to be a titan of art demands a special kind of sensibility, an energy. Such an artist needs to be infused with a passion and a belief in his own invincibility if he is to transcend his craft. When he does so, he enters that rare space occupied by titans. These extraordinary men bestow upon us what is unique in the annals of consciousness: that is, a deeper understanding of what it is to be human.

The greatest of all these artists, however, is Michelangelo. He stands before us like a colossus, the range of his work reaching beyond that of any other artist before his time, or since. We can marvel at Picasso's inventiveness and exuberance. We can admire the audacity of Turner as he plays with our sense of atmosphere.

We can even delight in Caravaggio's chiaroscuro that makes us want to reach out and touch his work. But all these are only examples of a majestic use of technique informed by a pure imagination. Yet, when it comes to understanding Michelangelo, we need to apply another yardstick altogether. He was not an artist so much as a man in league with the power of representation as a unifying signification. He did not want to sculpt or paint things as they are, but to make them more real than their capacity to be. In his hands the human figure reached beyond all previous attempts to stand alone as an object that we might admire, in order to become an embodiment of a physiological urgency which says to us that our torments and our aspirations are in some way a condition of spiritual growth. Michelangelo wanted us to find a new impetus to life through the intercession of our own desire to be better than who we are.

I make these observations in the full knowledge that I am treading on holy ground. Artists like Michelangelo are considered a part of the canon of excellence that we look to when we wish to express why art is so important to us as the foundation of our cultural life. To talk about them in such a manner is to inevitably resort to superlatives, because these in themselves protect the artist from any criticism. In so doing, we tell ourselves that men like Michelangelo live in an empirium of their own. They do not inhabit our world. They become the very touchstone of beauty and of excellence, the gods that preside over human expression for all eternity.

Titans are more than just artists, however. They do more than paint, sculpt, or design buildings, each according to their individual discipline – they do all of these together, and more. They are not content to create an original artwork, or carve a polished figure for their own sake; but rather, they want to place their imprimatur on every aspect of beauty, to show the world that what they contain within themselves knows no bounds. To pick up a brush or a chisel is the least important aspect of their chosen craft. What men like Michelangelo do is impose themselves upon a canvas, on a wall, or a block of stone as a gesture of defiance. This is the nature of their titanism. They become a force of nature in themselves.

It is hard, then, to come to terms with the fact that Michelangelo was also a great poet. How could this be so, one asks? Where did he find the time to fashion sonnets and madrigals when much of his time was spent in a Carrara quarry, among its towering edifices of bluish marble, hoping to find a particular block that he might fashion into a masterpiece. Or elsewhere, in a workshop in Florence or Rome furiously chipping away with mallet and chisel at the behest of Pope or prince. More importantly, how could an imagination such as his retreat so quickly from the concrete to the abstract in pursuit of the beauty that he craved? He was, as the old Florentine records tell us, *a master of live stone* for whom the very rocks seemed to have a life. It was a quality that he brought to his poetry also, many of which appear to have been carved from stone.

It is these aspects of his character that I wish to explore in this little book. Michelangelo as a poet is not someone we readily identify with because we want him to remain Promethean in his endeavours. In our eyes he is a big man. He is a man pummeled by the political instability of his time, by arrogant Popes obsessed with perpetuating themselves, by fawning friends eager to bathe in his aura, and by family members wishing to fleece him of his occasional wealth. There is nothing that is calm or ordered about Michelangelo's life. His passions, his acute sensibilities, and his willfulness often cloud his judgment. But through it all he is who he is – a towering figure that defies description, even at a time when huge personalities are commonplace in sixteenth - century Italy.

Michelangelo, the poet. It is hard to imagine those chapped hands of his picking up a quill of an evening to write words of such grace which actually say things, rather than merely expressing elegant thoughts. He hated the ornate Petrarchan style of his fellow poets, of course, even though he was strongly influenced by the great man himself. Francesco Berni, a comic poet of some note, famously said of his friend, referring to the work of another poet, 'he says things, while you speak words' *(ei dice cosa, e voi dite parole)*. Our admiration for Michelangelo is thus aroused by his ability to convey an infinity of spirit in his poetry, much as he did in his sculpture.

But a writer of love poetry? How could a man who made the heroic figure of *David* his exemplar fashion poetry dedicated to a woman? Yet he did so, late in his life, to a widow who was also a fair poet herself. Vittoria Colonna, the marchioness of Pescara (1492-1547), became the unlikely object of his affections when Michelangelo was already sixty-three and she forty-four years of age. Not a passionate relationship, clearly. But one that was to produce from his pen more than forty poems dedicated to his great love for the marchioness. For a man who neither married nor appeared to have had any permanent relationship other than with a number of his men friends, Italy's greatest artist nonetheless discovered something in this woman of mature years that fulfilled all his deepest yearnings.

It is necessary to reach back into Michelangelo's early childhood before we begin to understand why he resorted to poetry to express his feelings about love. Certainly, in his great works of sculpture and painting the theme of love is not overtly present. Even in his well-known Pietas in Bruges, Rome, and Florence, he does not address human love but the theme of divine love itself.So that somewhere in his early life Michelangelo did not experience a normal, nurturing love that we might expect. For reasons we do not know, he was put out to nurse with a stonecutter's wife in the village of Settignano owned by his father, Lodovico. The village was located near Fiesole, outside Florence.

We do not know much about Michelangelo's mother, Francesca Neri, other than she was nineteen at the time of his birth. Unlike his father, she is an anonymous presence in the young artist's life. Vasari refers to her only as 'the virtuous and noble wife of Lodovico', and Ascanio Condivi, another friend of Michelangelo, does not even mention her name. All we know from the lips of the artist himself is that the formative years of his early life were determined by the milk of a wet-nurse and the noise of mallet on chisel. 'If my brains are any good at all,' he told Giorgio Vasari later in life, 'it's because I was born in the pure air of your Arezzo countryside [near La Verna], just as with my mother's milk I sucked in hammer and chisels that I use for my statues.' Already we see him covering up the fact that his 'mother's milk' (or milk-mother) did not come from Francesca. He was the nursling of another woman, a stone-cutter's wife.[1]

Should we read into Michelangelo's remark any more than the ironic humour that he wished to impart? Did he see himself more as the child of a stone-cutter's wife than of Francesca, his mother, who died when he was six years old? In all his correspondence we see no mention of her name. His father and his brothers are often mentioned, however. Though we know that he had four brothers, it does suggest that his upbringing was entirely normal. His father, we are told, always had his best interests at heart, and finally accepted that the boy was a prodigy. Ludovico later remarried, and we do not know how Michelangelo viewed his stepmother. Though he received little formal schooling, and was often

---

1 According to Walter Pater *(The Renaissance)* Michelangelo spent his formative years with his

sickly as a child, Michelangelo soon found himself apprenticed to Domenico Ghirlandaio, a prominent fresco painter of Florence, a man of gentle disposition, in order to learn his trade with his father's blessing, at the age of fifteen.

During that time, another incident occurred which was to have a profound affect upon the young artist. Benevento Cellini tells us that when he and others were learning to draw in the Church of the Carmine while studying the work of Masaccio in one of its chapels, Michelangelo made a disparaging remark towards Piero Torrigiano, another young artist. Torrigiano became so incensed that he punched Michelangelo on the nose, breaking it badly. 'I felt bone and cartilage go down like biscuit beneath my knuckles,' he said. Michelangelo bore this disfigurement for the rest of his life. It must have been painful for him- he, who lived for the glory of physical beauty as being a demonstration of the divine.

Two important but disparate incidents in the life of an artist. It is hard to know how much Michelangelo was affected by them, though we do know that he became increasingly withdrawn in the years that followed. Perhaps he did feel marked by these seemingly insignificant events, we do not know. But what we do know is that

Michelangelo began to mistrust his fellow men as he matured, and to indulge in vindictiveness for no apparent reason whenever he felt himself slighted. In one of his longer poems written around 1450, he speaks to us of his own sense of isolation and aloneness:

> I am a poor man and alone
> A genii trapped in a bottle
> Or a pith in its rind, and
> My dark tomb affords me
> little chance to escape.

In that same poem he speaks of melancholy as his greatest joy, and aninability to love *(Fiamma d'amor nel cor non m'e rimasa)* because of the incapacity of his soul to do so. In his poetry Michelangelo was not averse to serious self - analysis, something that we do not attribute very often to artists of any period. For the most part they simply *are*, and do not display any great interest in self-reflection. But Michelangelo did so often, never pulling back either from self-disparagement. 'I find my happiness in melancholy,' he announced, loftily placing himself above happiness. This is the talk of a man who cannot find a way to be more than an artist, in spite of his longing to realize some spiritual revelation.

Nor did he paint or sculpt his self-portrait very often. When he did, as in the *Victory* statue in the Palazzo Vecchio in Florence (1533), where he portrayed himself on bended knee in a gesture of defeat, or as a person skinned alive by the poet Pietro Aretino in the *Last Judgment* as depicted in the Sistine Chapel ceiling, we see a man undone by his own self-doubt. Not as an artist, because he never doubted his talent, but as a solitary man, a man incapable of living a normal life in love. In a sketch of himself wearing the coif of a boar's head, we see a man embracing his own wildness, his own savagery, his broken nose an echo of a boar's snout. He never doubted that in some way he bore the mark of Cain upon his brow. He was an outsider, condemned to live only for his art in which he immersed himself in order to stave off a sense of lifelong ennui.

More importantly, as in the *Victory* statue, we gain an inkling into another sense of his own failings. The figure of Victory is an example of ideal masculine beauty, much of its upper shoulder stance similar to that of *David's*. Now a man in his late fifties, it is clear that Michelangelo regarded himself as a man defeated by beauty in that his own adolescent good looks had been taken from him in a brawl. What he has idolized all his life is now behind him as a man. He can celebrate it in a statue, as he had done many times, but in the end what he stood for in his own mind was in array.

We should be aware of how Michelangelo depicted himself in his own work. He never idolized himself as Raphael did on occasions, or as Durer did in his magnificent self-portraits in both Madrid and Munich. When we do see him in a line drawing or in an oil painting he is usually gazing back at us from deep within his own solitude. He is no Renaissance *uomo universale* or ideal man as so many other artists and writers wished to depict themselves. Michelangelo is the Suffering Man, a man in anguish. His is the broken visage of his age, the dark side of its illusory engagement with human perfection. Michelangelo knows his failings better than anyone.

Of course, Michelangelo longed for love and to be loved, particularly when he was a young man. There are lovers, all of them young men like himself, their features, their gestures, even sometimes their sensibilities, ever presenting him with the prospect of a long-term relationship. But it never really happened. Some left him because they grew tired of his importunities; others merely distanced themselves and allowed him to remain their friend such as Tommaso Cavaliere, a young Roman nobleman. He remarked once, 'Whenever I see someone who possessed some *virtu*, who displays some agility of mind, who knows how to do or say something more suavely than the rest, I am constrained to fall in love with him...' Even so, he admitted to having few genuine friends. As late as 1550, when he was already an old man, he could still remark to his nephew, Lionardo Buonarroti, 'As for beauty, you are scarcely the most handsome youth in Florence...' thereby silencing the young man, who at that point was looking for a wife with the help of his uncle. Beauty as a bargaining counter was ever present.

We are thus confronted by a man whose lack of insouciance belies that of his Age. There was something pervasively constrained about his character. We know that he much admired the writings of Savanarola, a firebrand Florentine preacher and religious reformer who railed against the corruption of the secular authorities in his city, as well as the Church in Rome. He was not the only artist to come under his influence; we know that Botticelli was deeply taken by his millennial prophesies and visions. Savonarola's influence on him as a young man set the tone of Michelangelo's pessimism towards political activity in general. More than anything, he hated tyrants.

So how did such a man find himself falling in love with a woman like Vittoria Colonna? The very idea of this event happening defies all our previous knowledge of his life. For a man who found it so difficult to endure the coquetries and madnesses of women, it seems hard to believe him finding solace in the company of one, let alone a widow of some mature years. Yet such an event did occur, possibly in Rome around 1538, where Michelangelo spent much of his later life working for the Papacy. Nothing in his previous life, however, suggested that a woman like Vittoria could enter his life and transform his understanding of love so radically. It is this part of his story that we must now begin to explore through a better understanding of the marchioness herself. For it is she who inspired him to write some of his greatest poetry, and it is to her that we must turn.[2]

---

[2] There is some suggestion that they may have met earlier, when Vittoria was nineteen, on the occasion of the opening of the Sistine Chapel in 1508 - 9, an occasion for man of the elite of Rome to attend. If this is so, they did not begin to know one another seriously until much later.

2

Vittoria Colonna draws near to us through a veil of history and privilege. Considered to be one of the most beautiful women in the Italy of her day, and along with her good friend Giulia Gonzaga, she was a representative of a new breed of enlightened women prepared to add their own footnote to the pages of history. She did so not because of her elevated place in Roman society, but because of the power of her intellect. Vittoria, like Giulia, stand before us as an example of a true Renaissance woman. Beautiful, elegant, highly cultured, well educated, few men could match either of them in the art of persuasion or argument.

Born in 1490 in the castle of Marino outside Rome, Vittoria was the daughter of Fabrizzio Colonna, Grand Constable of Naples by his marriage to Agnesinia di Montifeltro, daughter of Frederigo, Duke of Urbino. Blood more illustrious than hers could not be found in all Italy.

At four years old her parents betrothed her to Ferrante Francesco d'Avalos, a boy of the same age, the only son of the Marchese di Pescara. This marriage was suggested by Ferrante II, the King of Sicily and Naples, who desired to see an alliance between the powerful house of Colonna and one of the chief Spanish families then settled in Italy. At nineteen Vittoria and Ferrante were married in an elaborate ceremony in Ischia, the fief and residence of the house of d'Avalos. On Vittoria's side it was definitely a love-match, one that she was to honour throughout her life, in spite of her husband's infidelities and frequent absences on military campaign.

Ferrante was destined for a brilliant military career if death had not cut it short. Early in their marriage he fought numerous battles against the invading French, culminating in the defeat of Italian forces at Ravenna in 1512. He was wounded and briefly made a prisoner until a large ransom was paid for his release. During his time in captivity he nonetheless managed to write a *Dialogo d'Amore* to his wife back in Ischia, to which she replied with an equally mannered *Epistola*. One senses that the young couple wanted to make a go of their marriage against all the odds.

As general of the Imperial forces, Ferrante spent the next few years in perpetual military operations, until he finally overcame the French at Pavia in 1525. During those years Vittoria rarely saw him. Little did she know that he had fallen into the trap of political skullduggery, which lead him to betray his own side to Charles V. in the hope of receiving the crown of Naples.[3] He might have entered Naples in triumph had he not fallen ill and died suddenly a few months later. Accused of double treachery and being a traitor, we have to assume that Ferrante lost his footing in the conflicting currents of Italian politics.[4] It is said that when Vittoria heard of his death at Viterbo, while she was riding to his bedside from Rome at his request, she fell from her horse and remained for two hours in a semi-comatose condition.

Burdened with her husband's guilt, which she was well aware of, Vittoria never abandoned her

---

3   He had earlier besmirched his reputation by allowing his troops to mercilessly sack Como, after agreeing to spare the city in the campaign of 1521 against French forces. He did so again in 1522 after besieging Genoa. Nonetheless he gained a reputation of being the ablest and mostenterprising of the Imperial generals. (Prescott, *History of Charles V*)

4   The historian Guicciardini said of Ferrante, 'There was no one in Italy of more malignity or ofless good faith than the Marchese.' *(History of Italy)*. Another historian, Ripamonte, pro-nounced a similar verdict: 'There was not to be found in his day any one more deeply dyed in perfidity, or more courageous in arms.'

loyalty and love for Ferrante, even in death.⁵ She wrote many poems honouring his memory in the ensuing years, perhaps because she wanted to preserve their young and fervent love from history's verdict. It was a difficult time for Vittoria. A young widow without child, her husband's reputation clouded by treason, there was little left for her to do other than to dedicate herself to his memory and to religion. Her only joy was to be found in the upbringing of Ferrante's young nephew and heir, the Marchese Francesco del Vasto. She managed to make of this headstrong young man a person of some considerable culture, before his own untimely death at forty-two in North Africa fighting against Barbary pirates.⁶

We are left in the presence of a woman whose hopes of living a happy conjugal life

---

5 Heath Wilson wrote in his *Life of Michelangelo,* 'Vittoria wept for him (Ferrante); none could judge better than she, with her clear, moral perceptions, of his errors, but her affection for him never failed, and after his death she remembered only his brilliant qualities and their mutual happiness.'

6 An affable man, much loved by his adopted mother Vittoria, Alfonso d'Avalos del Vasto, Marquis of Pescara (1502-46), was described as 'a handsome man, and exceedingly gallant; very particular as to his dress, and whether at peace or at war, made so strong a use of perfumes that even his horse's saddle smelt of essences.' (Brantome) He died of a fever in 1546, a year before the marchioness, after falling out of favor with Charles V.

had been dashed. In her despair she begged to be taken to a convent and given the nun's habit. Her brother Ascanio, hearing of her plight, hastened to her side in Viterbo in order to bring her back to Rome. There she took up residence in the Convent of San Silvestro, with which her family had been connected since the thirteenth-century. The convent was in the hands of the order of Santa Chiara where one of her ancestors had previously taken the veil. Perhaps Vittoria had secretly wanted to emulate her illustrious predecessor, Princess Margherita, who had taken a vow of poverty and daily begged for alms in the street until her early death and beatification by Pius IX.

Vittoria Colonna retired into what she knew. Widowhood suited her, as it allowed her to concentrate on her spiritual life, her broad range of intellectual friends, and her responsibilities as a woman of noble birth. She conducted a wide correspondence with illustrious men of letters as well as a group of thinkers in the vanguard of the counter Reformation in Italy. Though she never adopted Protestantism herself, and always remained deeply orthodox in her Catholic belief, Vittoria was never afraid to speak her mind, which of course aroused suspicions in the Holy Office. Her principal interest was in bringing the Church back to a purer morals and sincerity of faith, so that the Church might undergo a regeneration from within.

It is well to hear her voice expressing her love of Christ. She is not mystical in any way, but she does favour a deeply felt piety, a quality we rarely hear of today. In a letter that she wrote to her dear friend, the poet Gaspara Stampa living in the Convent of Sao Paolo in Milan, we gain a sense of how she embraced the profound adventure of the spiritual life:

> I love you and will love you always, if you will love Him who loves you so much; and not only through my letters, but with my blood, my soul, my life.... I pray you to familiarize yourself by constant thought with the pains and torments that have been suffered by you. Take some time from your other occupations to spend it at the feet of your Saviour. Pray do this, so that you may be made worthy to receive true light and real knowledge of the will of God in you, so that you may be able to perform it, and pray for me.

It is not the voice of an Angela of Foligno or indeed of a Therese of Avila that we hear, great mystical writers as both of them were. But is it a sincere voice of piety that we hear. We are at once alerted to how Vittoria regarded herself as being a woman of a certain kind of unworldliness blessed with the gift of making goodness seem attractive. This made her very appealing to those who knew her. She rarely judged people; her real interest lay in celebrating how important it was to aspire to a high cast of character, as well as a true appreciation of those things worth striving for.

Her friendships were wide-ranging and long-standing, nor was she immune from dispensing flattery if it served her purpose. All her talent as a writer could be brought to bear, thus making some of her letters to friends perfect embellishments in themselves. In a letter to Baldassare Castiglione, the celebrated author of *The Courtier*, she succeeded in laying claim to a copy of his book that he had asked her to return, with these well constructed words:

> ... I have never seen, nor expect to see, another work in prose superior to this, or to be compared with it; nor, perhaps, one that deserves to be ranked second to it. Because of the new and beautiful subject, the excellence of the style is such that, with a sweetness never felt before, it leads you to a charming and fruitful hill, ascending always, without ever letting you perceive that you are no longer on the plain where you entered... Nor do I think that such jewels can be found, nor any artificer to improve on their setting.

Could Castiglione ever have had the courage to insist on his book's return after these witty and flattering remarks? Not likely! Vittoria's gift for making her friends feel special was consummate. She later wrote a similar letter to Michelangelo in order to obtain a sketch of the Crucifixion from his hand. Once more her careful artistry of expression came to the fore when she wrote to the artist: 'I have received your letter and examined the Crucifixion which has certainly crucified in my mind all other picture that I have ever seen etc.' A need to possess what was great by another suggests her desire to feel their greatness as a part of herself.[7]

It was critical to being who she was. The love of friendship was important to her, as it was to many of her era. For Vittoria, it was rightly considered to be the most ethereal and spiritual of loves between two people. Friendship implied equality, something that Vittoria was at pains to cultivate in all her fraternal relationships. The tone and style of her writing was always those of a great princess, thus ensuring the elevated position that she and many of her class cultivated.

---

[7] Castiglione later complained that Vittoria had leant the book to too many people, that a great part of it had been transcribed for others. It prompted him to hurriedly publish the book after it had languished for ten years in his study. Before he died, however, he wrote a letter of apology to the marchioness. It is said that Castiglione wrote *The Courtier* as much to please her as his royal patron, Louis XII of France.

Nonetheless, she invariably showed exquisite respect towards her correspondents, including Michelangelo. 'Magnificent Messer Michelangelo' or 'Unique Messer Michelangelo, and my singular friend', were only some of the honorifics that she used when addressing the artist.

Her letters to him, we are told, Michelangelo treasured long after her death, 'breathing honourable and tender affections' upon them. The rough and ready demeanor of the artist was somehow softened in her presence, or when a letter arrived from Viterbo where she often went to pass the summer. Moreover, her proficiency in poetry, her knowledge of art and literature, and her cultivated mind, must have made her companionship delightful to all those who knew her. Contrition, humility, and unwavering faith informed everything she did. Though Vittoria was no saint, lacking perhaps the quality of abandon that characterized so many female saints of her time, she nonetheless conveyed a tenderness that endeared her to most.

In spite of her status as a noble, Vittoria was known to walk about Rome unrecognized and in the poorest of clothes *(abito abietissimo)*, possibly in a bid to emulate Princess Margherita, her forebear. While she was living in San Silvestro in

Rome she rarely received visitors, preferring to live the commonlife with the nuns. One of her close associates at that time was Sienese-born Bernardino Ochino, a mystic and preacher who became popular in Rome and Naples.[8] It was during one of his visits to Naples that he met with Vittoria, who urged him to take up arms against the infidel in Palestine, hoping that he might undertake a Crusade so that she might accompany him on a pilgrimage to the holy sites herself. Nothing came of it; but her fervor does indicate a desire on her part to participate in some glorious moment. She eventually broke with Ochino, probably with great sadness, after he became a Protestant and fled to Zurich, thence to England, for fear of being arrested by the Inquisition.[9] It seems that Vittoria was always sailing close to the wind with regard to her Christian beliefs. Clearly, Protestantism did hold out some attraction to her, even if she lost some friends along the way.

---

8   Fra. Bernardino of Siena. He was a Capuchin monk so earnest and eloquent in his preaching that is was said that he could melt the very stones to tears.

9   Ochino found asylum in England, where he was made a prepend of Canterbury Cathedral. He later received a pension from Edward VI's privy purse, and composed his major work, the *Tragoedie or Dialoge of the unjuste usurped primacie of the Bishop of Rome*. He was an advocate of polygamy.

Her position as a poet was much vaunted by her contemporaries, including Ariosto, who mentioned her in his *Orlando Furioso*. There he praised her for her 'sweet style', strong words from the great man. On the whole, however, Vittoria's work is constrained, lacking the passionate voice of the true poet. Her best poetry is reserved for religious themes such as the sonnets she wrote in *The Triumph of the Cross*. She also penned a number of poems in praise of the Holy Virgin in which she was able to open her heart to what she called 'supernal Love' *('l'amor superno)*. A few lines from one of her sonnets give us a taste of her verse:

> From joy to joy, from one to other band
> Of sweet and gentle thoughts, supernal Love
> From the hard winter and the cold thereof
> Guides me to spring's warm and verdant land.
>
> Happily the Lord – since he beholds me stand
> With breast like wax whereon the eternal seal
> Has deeply cut a faith profound and real,
> Moulding my innermost heart beneath His hand.[10]

Her voice is one of deep piety, not of any mystical insight such as one might find in Francis' *Hymn to the Sun* or the *Lauds* of Jacapone of Todi. Both these poets drew upon nature to enliven their verse, something that Vittoria did not do. Per-

---

10   *Vittoria Colonna,* Maud F. Jerrold. New York: J.M. Dent and Co.,1906

haps nature did not mean as much to her as it did to them. But she would have concurred with Jacapone's remark when he wrote to Brother John of La Verna, who was then passing a winter shivering with cold and in fever: 'I have always held and still do, that it is a great thing to be filled with God. Why? Because humility is then wedded to reverence. But I have always thought, and still do, that to know how to suffer His absence, how to endure that fast when He imposes it, is even greater. Why? Because faith is then attested to without witnesses, hope without expectation of reward, charity without signs of benevolence. Such are the foundations of the holy hills. They lead to that summit where rocks have the sweetness of honey and stone the savor of the finest oil.' One senses that Vittoria Colonna would have understood these sentiments perfectly.[11]

Though we possess numerous portraits of the marchioness, more notably one by Sebastiano del Piombo, which portray her as the great beauty that she was, we only have a few pencil drawings of her by Michelangelo.[12] One of these is a strange

---

11   Jacapone da Todi, *The Lauds*. Paulist Press: New York, 1982.

12   Michelangelo is reputed to have painted a portrait of Vittoria, however, along with his othergreat love, Tommaso Cavaliere, neither of which is extent. We do have pencil studies of both.

little drawing, almost a caricature, as he has depicted Vittoria in a state of old age with sagging breasts. Her eyes are lowered in the presence of himself wearing his boar's head coif. What was he thinking when he made these drawings? He, an aging man dressed up like a shaman from the north; she, barely in contact with her body. All pretense has been stripped away. It is as if Michelangelo wanted to confront the reality of who they were: a princess shorn of her beauty, and a broken-faced sculptor reverting to his animaline origin. Both images are a far cry from the two people who figure so largely in his poems.

Of course, there is a misogynistic element to Michelangelo's character. He had no particular love for women in general, and when he painted or drew them, as he did in the Sistine Chapel or in his pencil studies of Cleopatra, Venus, and Leda, we are confronted by a series of tableaus of men disguised as women. This may seem like a harsh judgment, but we need to ask ourselves why this great artist and sculptor wished to depict women in such a masculine way. I have asked myself this question many times. The nude male body he loved; the female body for the most part he clothed. The only time when he truly depicted the Feminine in all its ethereal beauty was in the Pieta in Rome, as well as in the Bruges Pieta. Both images of the Madonna transcend their physical appearance to embrace a quality of the purely feminine.

Such a strange friendship, then, such an extraordinary love between two people of quite different backgrounds. I try to imagine what drew them together in the first place, what inspired them when they first met that day in Rome. A noble lady, an *altezza* no less, and an ordinary man, a rough sculptor from the provinces, with only a rudimentary education who happened also to be a genius, these two people had somehow found in one another a capacity to love outside the normal constraints of their class.

Between Michelangelo and Vittoria a tender affection soon sprung up based upon their ardent and high-seeking natures. If love be the right word to describe their fervid attachment, then it seems that both of them released in one another forces of the heart that had been long pent-up. For all his artistic Platonism, one senses that Michelangelo saw in Vittoria someone who would not judge him nor call him to account for his strange and quixotic lifestyle. His liking for young men of course she would have known about; but in no way did Vittoria allow any gossip to come between them. Her serenity, in a way, re-manned him, made him feel his wholeness at last.

For her part, Vittoria wanted to engage in a loving friendship that was both Platonic and well meant. A strange combination, but one that suited her desire to remain attractive to a genius such as Michelangelo. In a way, she idolized him as the supreme artist. His portrayal of the Virgin Mother in the Rome Pieta (known as the *Madonna della Febbre*) must have struck her as one of unequalled edification: a woman, a divine mother, announced herself to the world as eternally youthful, the bearer of Christ as God's greatest gift to the world. At least, this is how Vittoria might have regarded his Pieta. She saw in Michelangelo a man whose piety was more than a match for her own. And he saw in her, perhaps, a figure of his milk mother that went back to the time of his infancy near Florence.

3

Michelangelo lived at a time of great intellectual ferment in Italy. Florence, where he studied and worked as a young man of fifteen, was home to some of the most brilliant men in all Europe. Under the wise patronage of Lorenzo de' Medici, the defacto tyrant of Florence, these men presided over a vital new impetus in philosophy and in letters. Because Lorenzo cultivated and admired the young Michelangelo, and regularly invited him to sit by his side at the family table, the artist found himself listening to conversations between men that would ultimately determine the future of philosophic inquiry during the period we now know as the Renaissance. There was no better place, it seems, for this young prodigy to begin his education than in the company of such men.

It is well to know who some of these thinkers were. If we begin with Lorenzo himself, we are in the presence of a unique individual, the perfect *uomo universale*. He presided over his tiny nation-state at a moment when political institutions were everywhere inclining to despotism, and when the spiritual life of his countrymen founds its noblest expression in art and literature. He was a man of marvelous variety and range of mental power. His mercurial nature perfectly fitted him for the task of being all things to all men. To a philosopher he passed for a sage, among men of letters he was an original and graceful poet, among Greek scholars he was sensitive to ever nicety of the Attic idiom, and among artists he was seen as an amateur gifted with a refined discernment and consummate taste.

While he enjoyed the reputation of being a libertine, who could dance and masquerade with the merriest, he was also the author of devotional lauds and mystery plays, a profound theologian and a critic of sermons. He was as good a judge of cattle as he was of statues. This made him an ideal candidate to resuscitate culture in his city, even if he chose to ignore its religious and constitutional liberties. Florence, he believed, needed a wise patron not a protector of the polity.

His teacher was Marsilio Ficino, the founder of the Platonic Academy in the gardens of Careggi near Fiesole where he and others used to gather to discuss philosophic topics. Ficino was the most learned man of his age. Like Michelangelo, he had entered the Medicean household at the behest of Lorenzo's father, Cosimo, in order to continue his studies in Greek and Latin. His health was delicate and his sensibilities acute; his intellect, we are told, inclined towards mysticism and theology, which fitted him well for the task of unifying religion with philosophy. He was no pagan, however, and at the age of forty he took holy orders.

At forty-four, Ficino completed the translation of Plato's works into Latin. This was an important event in the history of Renaissance thought. He later wrote a life of the Greek philosopher, and a treatise on the *Platonic Doctrine of Immortality*. This book formed the basis of many of the discussions held at Villa Careggi by those of the Medicean circle, which included the young Michelangelo, along with Botticelli and other artists favored by Lorenzo. The summer of an Italian sky presided over these remarkable gatherings each year, where men such as Cristoforo Landino, Angelo Politiziano, Leo Battista Alberti, Luigi Pulci, and the refined young philosopher Giovanni di Mirandola, all gathered by the rose bushes, there to cement the name of Florence as the new Athens of the Age.

Pico di Mirandola was perhaps one of the most interesting of this group. As Poliziano remarked of this young man of princely birth, 'Nature seemed to have showered on this young man, or hero, all her gifts.' His face had something of divinity shining from it. Indeed, his mother observed a strange circular flame on the wall where she lay giving birth to her son that suddenly vanished, which bestowed upon her a presentiment of his future fame. His memory was prodigious, and in his studies he was indefatigable. It is hard to know whether his talents or his moral qualities conferred on him the greater lustre. His personal attractions made him the idol of Florentine society, not least of young women, and it is no surprise that Lorenzo included him in his inner circle; he was, so to speak, the jewel in its crown.[13]

When Michelangelo was eleven years old Pico published his famous nine hundred theses in Rome, defending Platonic mysticism. It was an important moment in the freeing up of thought from the dead hand of Church stricture. Though Pico was sharply criticized by the Vatican, and briefly excommunicated, there was no going back. He had opened the way for Greek thought,

---

13   Pico was born in 1463 in Mirandola, and did not come to Florence until he was twenty years old.

Plato and Plotinus' in particular, to inform the exciting new ideas that contributed to the fruition the greatness of Renaissance art.

Michelangelo, ever the recipient of new ideas from wherever they might come, must have enjoyed the intellectual fervor of those days when he, too, entered the Medicean circle at a young age. The genii was out of the bottle: he could begin to sculpt and draw like one blessed with fresh eyes in seeing the beauty that surrounded him. He, more than any artist of his time, embraced Platonic mysticism as the scaffold of his future work. That Pico died too young did not mean that his various forays into ancient literature, including the Jewish Cabbala, had not found fertile ground in the mind of young Michelangelo.[14]

Ficino presided over this ferment. He encouraged men like Alberti to expound on his revolutionary theories about architecture. Landino tells us of a few days they all spent in the hill-set sanctuary of Saint Romualdo in the Casentino region. Lorenzo joined many noble youths of Florence to meet and hear Alberti speak about the

---
14 A women friendly to Savonarola, when she first met Pico in Florence, prophesized that he was too beautiful to live long, and would die prematurely, in the 'time of the lilies', signifying a withering of those flowers in the heat of summer. He died on the 17th November 1494, the very day the French entered Florence, with the lilies of France on their shields.

'theoretical life' *(bios theoretikos)*, expounding his thesis on Plato with a charm and eloquence peculiar to himself. Solitude and meditation, as well as communing with nature, he maintained, are the true nurses of great spirits. Lorenzo, however, countered with his argument about the 'practical life' *(bios praktikos)* as a necessary adjunct to the development of self-culture. The philosopher must descend from his high place and mix with men in order to exercise those faculties matured by contemplation.

Michelangelo was not yet born when this debate took place; it occurred a year before. But the arguments that were made that day would have quickly circulated around Florence and become common knowledge. Landino had taken the trouble of recording their conversations in his Latin work, *Camaldolese Discussions,* for others to read and comment upon. Since Michelangelo's Latin was at best rudimentary, he would have only heard of its contents from others. But this did not mean that the young artist was immune to its influence. Moreover, one suspects that he learnt a great deal from hearing Alberti talk about architecture on other occasions when they met. His own work as the architect and designer of St Peter's dome in Rome later in his career was likely informed by hearing Alberti speak at different times.

Poliziano was another significant influence on the young Michelangelo. He had been a tutor to Lorenzo's children in the Medici Palace, and so would have guided the young artist in his studies, or when they broke bread together at Lorenzo's table. A born poet, Poliziano entered Lorenzo de 'Medici's circle on Ficino's recommendation, and went on to become one of the greatest scholars of his age. He wrote Latin as if it were a living language. More than anyone, he realized what many Italians had been striving for – the rebirth of antiquity in the life of a man of the modern world. Among his translations were the work of Epictetus, Galen, Plutarch, and the *Charmides* of Plato. He celebrated Virgil with the same panache as he did Homer. Rather more pagan than Christian, Poliziano rather ingratiated himself with Lorenzo, and so lost some respect for his achievements. Before his death two years after his benefactor, he wrote a short lament to Lorenzo that prophesized his own eclipse:

> Oh, that my head were waters
> My eyes a fountain of tears
> So that I might cry day and night!
> So mourns the widowed turtle dove
> As does the dying swan
> Followed by the nightingale.

Was it also a lament for the imminent death of a great age? Shortly after his death the deluge prophesized by Savonarola burst upon Italy, and the light of humanism was all but dimmed.

Nothing had quite the impact on humanist thought, however, than Pico's *Oration on the Dignity of Man*. It was published in 1486, when Michelangelo was barely eleven years old. Nothing like it had ever been written before, even by the ancient philosophers themselves. In the *Oration* Pico writes that 'human vocation is a mystical vocation that has to be realized following a three stage way, which comprehends necessarily moral transformation, intellectual research, and final perfection in the identity with the absolute reality. This paradigm is universal, because it can be retraced in every tradition.'[15] Uniquely so, Pico drew upon Christian writers, the Jewish Cabbala, and the glosses of Arab philosophers in order to make his point – that man is the interpreter of nature. He was, in many ways, the first universalist writer of the Renaissance.

Nor did he abandon his interest in the old gods for the sake of his Christian belief. This wandering philosopher of great sensitivity and grace,

---

15 From *The Portable Renaissance Reader*, edit. James Bruce Ross and Mary Martin McLaughlin. New York: Penguin Books, 1977.

who had travelled all over Europe in search of knowledge, established the primacy of the intellect as a spiritual condition rather than an intellectual one – and all this before he had reached the age of twenty-five! His *Oration* can be seen as the true manifesto of the Renaissance:

> You who are confined by no limits, shall determine for yourself your own nature, in accordance with your own free will, in whose hands I have placed you. I have set you at the centre of the world, so that from there you may more easily survey whatever is in the world. We have made you neither heavenly nor earthly, neither mortal nor immortal, so that, more freely and more honourably the moulder and maker of yourself, you may fashion yourself in whatever form you shall prefer.[16]

It is hard to gauge the significance of such a treatise on the young mind of Michelangelo when he first read it. What we do know is that he soaked up this heady brew of Platonism with the fervor of a convert. By the time he had sculpted *Bacchus* in 1496, all trace of Gothic medievalism had been erased from western art. Moreover, when his *David* burst upon Florence a few years later, carved from a faulty piece of marble that no previous sculptor would touch, the transfor-

---

16 Ibid.

mation was complete.[17] Ancient Greece had been brought back to life in the consciousness of Italians in a way that few artists could begin to emulate.

David embodied Pico's *Oration* perfectly, and gave to it a palpable reality because it suggested the future, not the past. In this respect we see *David* in a pose before he did battle with Goliath, not after his victory. This more than echoed Pico's words, which asked men to be better than who they were. The Renaissance had come into its own as a spiritual and philosophic reality at last.

All these men helped to change Michelangelo from a youthful rustic into a young man of considerable intellect. He became a child of his age who went on to stamp his impress upon it with some of the most remarkable studies in the history of western art. When we gaze up at his figures in the Sistine Chapel, we are at once confront-

---

17   It is said that the block of marble had lain abandoned for twenty-five years under the *loggia* of Orcagna in Florence. Michelangelo was asked whether he might be able to do something with it, and he agreed. Such was the uneven cut of the block that he was permitted to carve hands and other extremities if he so needed, and attach them to his work. Michelengelo refused: he wanted the stone to reveal what was imbedded in it in all its wholeness. The statue was unveiled in Piazza Signorelli in 1504 after a journey through the streets of Florencehauled by forty men, when Michelangelo was twenty-nine years old. See Appendix.

ed by his robust sibyls and sages, his prophets and fleshly cherubims, all of them partaking of an idealized physicality never witnessed before. The images above us are less a celebration of Biblical events as they are a cornucopia of extenuating human gestures. The world that Michelangelo offers us is not hagiography any more. The great fresco is, rather, where men and women are deeply engaged in enacting the human condition as they grapple with one of the least understood attributes of their age – that of *dignitas*.

Michelangelo was around thirty-six when he completed the ceiling frescoes. Though never a painter from his point of view, his dynamic energy nonetheless had been put to work on one of the masterpieces of the Italian Renaissance. He was no longer the young man who had carved the Rome Pieta, however. That man once regarded the Holy Virgin as consistent with the serenity that he possessed. But it was not to last. His idea of the chaste woman as depicted in the Pieta was not something that he readily identified with in real life. Indeed, Michelangelo was ever the solitary man in his dealings with the world. On the unlikely prospect of ever getting married, he was adamant: 'I have too much of a wife, and that is this art, which has already given me tribulations, and my children will be the works I leave behind.'[18]

This was the man who was yet to embrace love as anything more than a passing obsession, but an obsession nonetheless. It is probably no accident that Michelangelo identified with Tityus, the Greek giant who assaulted Leto on her way to the shrine at Delphi. Though her son Apollo quickly intervened to save her, and to condemn Tityus to be staked out in the underworld where his entrails might be gorged upon by vultures, in contrast Michelangelo's life was to be ever one of retribution for his own unsated passions, the torture of immoderate love, particularly toward young Tommaso Cavalieri to which this drawing was offered as a gift. Homo-eroticism caused the artist much suffering in his life, to the point where he attempted to assuage his guilt in many of his poems. In one of his uncompleted sonnets, written in 1524 when he was nearly fifty years old, we hear his anguish:

> Flee Love, lovers, flee the fire
> Its burn is fierce, its wound mortal;
> After love's first assault nothing avails,
> Neither strength or reason nor escape.

---

18   Giorgio Vasari, *Lives of the Artists*. London: Penguin Books, 1971.

> Flee, with no small example at hand
> Of Love's deadly arm and pointed arrow;
> Observe in me what evil will be yours
> The cruel and piteous game that it be.
>
> Flee, do not linger, at the first glance;
> I thought at any time I could dismiss him;
> Now I suffer, and you see how I burn.

Yet, deep within his character, there were dormant aspirations that no young man could possibly appease, in spite of his self-abasement. Michelangelo wanted something more – contact with a person that transcended the carnal so that he might begin to articulate his own frustrated belief in the divine as the primary impetus to his life. He was nothing if not a failed mystic: his only way of expressing how he felt at a metaphysical level, the level he had been schooled to understand in Florence as a young man, was by pouring his energies into the realization of beauty on canvas or in marble. Such was his frustration that he often turned to poetry to release his anxieties.

The change came for him when he was already an old man. At sixty-three Vittoria Colonna came into his life. One begins to sense that she was his last hope of finding enduring love. We do not know how they actually met; but what we do know is that she opened his heart to the prospect of sharing a mutual love of Christ. Both were deeply religious. What Vittoria brought to their relationship was something he had not experienced before, yet had always projected onto his young men friends in days past: that is, inviolability. As a widow of many years and a woman who had suffered, Vittoria radiated a quality of sanctity that had been missing in his life.

For the first time, it seemed, he did not need to touch someone, whether with his hands or his thoughts. It was a plea that he had to himself many years before in a madrigal, where he wrote: 'Oh God, oh God, oh God!/How can he reach my very heart/who seems not to touch me?' In a rather strange way, the marchioness reminded him of Mary Magdalene at the foot of the Cross: she was there to comfort him in his own suffering. In turn, he endowed her with an almost religious sublimity, and so worshipped her without fear of being considered a madman.

4

Michelangelo addressed his first poem to Vittoria Colonna in 1536, the same year that they met. In it he expressed a certain relief that he was able to speak to her with such openness, such frankness, something that his poems to Tommaso Cavalieri, for example, did not reflect. 'Truly, my lady, though divine in beauty/you act like any mortal being' represented the beginning of a new phase in his life. Moreover, he was able to reveal deep admiration for a woman for the first time. Until now his love poetry had been conflicted, often embroiled in illicit passion, personal torment, and suffering. He had found it difficult to rise above his own disbelief in himself. 'Ah, restore me to myself, that I may die,' was how he addressed Cavalieri as a mark of his despair.

We do not know what words were exchanged between these two people at their first meeting. All we can surmise is that they talked about art, about poetry perhaps, certainly about their mutual regard for one another. He would have been aware of her reputation as a woman of high culture, and of the circumstances surrounding the death of her husband. We do know that early in their friendship gifts were exchanged, along with letters of thanks. One of these gifts was a drawing that Michelangelo had made of the Crucifixion, now in the British Museum.

Michelangelo had hoped to deliver the drawing to her in person, it seems, but some untoward event had made that impossible. Nor did he wish to make Cavaliere their go-between, as the letter implies. Surely he would have liked to experience her pleasure when she gazed upon the drawing for the first time, but this did not happen. The 'great work' that he mentions in passing might well have been his carving of the tomb of Julius, one of the enduring frustrations of his career.[19] Instead he wrote to her to express his disappointment. We sense his urgency with regard to his affection for the marchioness:

> Signora Marchesa,
> As I am in Rome, there seems to be no need to leave the Crucifix to Messer Tommaso, and to make him an intermediary between your Ladyship and me, your servant, for me to serve you, and especially

---

19 The tomb was not completed until 1545, thirty-two years after it was first conceived. Condivi referred to it as the 'tragedy of the tomb'.

as I have desired to do more for you than for anyone I have ever known in the world. But the great work, of which I have been much occupied, has prevented your Ladyship from knowing this. And because I know that you know that love needs no master, and that he who loves sleeps not, still less were any intermediaries needed. And it seems as if I have forgotten that I was doing something I had not mentioned because I had planned a surprise. But my purpose has been frustrated: *mal fa chi tanta fe si tosto oblia.*

Your Ladyship's obedient servant,

Michelangelo Buonarroti in Rome.

To which Vittoria replies with all her witty yet heartfelt words:

Unique Messer Michelangelo,
And my most singular friend,

I have received your letter and examined the Crucifixion which has certainly crucified in my mind all other pictures that I have ever seen. Nor could one find another figure more beautifully designed, more living, and more finished. Truly I cannot express how subtly and how marvelously it is done. For this reason, I have made up my mind that it is from no other hand but yours, therefore enlighten me; if it belongs to another. If it is yours, however, I must have it at all costs… And if it is really yours, be patient, I shall never send it back to you. I have examined it carefully in the light, and with a lens and a mirror, and I have never seen a more perfect thing.

Yours to command,
The Marchesa of Pescara.

Such is the talk of two people aware of what they mean to one another. Though filled with conventional courtesies, other forces are clearly at work beneath the surface of their exchange. We are at once made aware that the drawing of the Crucifixion is at the heart of their correspondence: it binds them to one another because it implies a respect for their mutual piety. Michelangelo is pleading with the marchioness to receive his drawing as a measure of his love for her as a practicing believer like himself. He has poured his love of God into the drawing, and now, finally, there is someone who appreciates the intensity of his belief. As Vittoria observes: 'I have never seen a more perfect thing.' Someone has reached into his heart, and understands who he is.

In a later letter to Michelangelo, after he had given her a drawing of the *Deposition from the Cross,* in which the body of Christ is supported by two angels, while the Holy Virgin seated at the foot of the Cross stretched her arms upward to heaven, in which Vittoria expresses her own faith in helping Michelangelo to realize what she regards as a possessing 'goodness to things already perfect.' She writes, 'I had the greatest faith in God that he would grant you a supernatural grace to make this Christ. And when I saw it, it was so wonderful that it surpassed all my expectations in every way.' She goes on to conclude her letter by saying, '…it rejoices me greatly that the angel on the right hand should be so much more beautiful, because Michael will place you, Michelangelo, at the right hand of the Lord one day.'

Such a letter perfectly expresses how Vittoria wished to encourage the artist. Playing upon his name and the Archangel Michael, she is able to reveal her feelings for him, a man much older than herself who nonetheless had had overcome so many obstacles in his life, thus allowing Michelangelo to believe in himself again. In contrast, there was so much about the man whose work was a testimony to his genius that appealed to a noble woman such as herself. His integrity, yes, and his firm religious faith which echoed Vittoria's own, these would have made him extremely attractive to her. Michelangelo, too, would have admired the quietness and austerity of Vittoria's self-chosen life, living in a monastery. Her life was filled with broad spaces and long silences as a result. That these alleviated her sorrow made it possible for Vittoria to place a consecrating hand upon his shoulder, thus enriching him with her sympathy. As the poet Swinburne wrote, he saw the Godhead in her face.

Nor was Michelangelo the only person to recognize Vittoria Colonna's unique qualities. Another friend of hers, Fortunato Martinengo, who often used to visit the marchioness when he was in Rome, wrote of her, 'She is a wonderful and unique woman, and, for what I have been able to understand, on fire with the love of Christ... What humility is hers, and what unexampled goodness!'[20]

Michelangelo's response to Vittoria's generous overtures was to begin writing sonnets and madrigals in her honour. After the marchioness sent him some devotional paintings as gifts, along with two sonnets of her own, Michelangelo replied with a well composed letter. The letter reflects his new ability to express his long-suppressed religious feelings, something that cannot be found in any of his correspondence with others. It was as if Vittoria had given him permission to raise his thoughts to another level; he could now say what he felt without fear or favour.

> Because I took possession of the things your Ladyship has many times wished to give me, in order to receive them as little unworthily as I could, I desired, Lady, to make something for you from my own hand. Now, however, seeing and recognizing the grace of God cannot be bought and to keep it

---

20   A painting of the count is in the National Museum, London. It was painted around 1542.

> waiting is a grievous sin, I acknowledge my fault, and willingly accept your said gifts. And when I possess them, not because I shall have them in my house, but because I shall be *in* their house, I shall seem to be in Paradise....

To reinforce the contents of his letter, Michelangelo included one of his most beautiful sonnets with his missive:

> High lady, to be less unworthy of the gift
> Of your immense courtesy, at first
> My lowly mind tried wholeheartedly
> To reciprocate in kind.
>
> Knowing that my own powers can make
> No headway in achieving such a goal,
> I ask your forgiveness at my boldness
> So that my faults grow constantly wiser.
>
> I see clearly how wrong my belief
> is That my fleeting and frail acts can match
> Your divine grace raining down on me.
>
> Mind, skill, and memory give way: mortal
> As I am I can't repay your heavenly gift,
> Not even if I tried a thousand times.

At once we are in the presence of a man who has found a new outlet for his creativity. It was in part confessional, of course; but at another level it was therapeutic. For a man who found it difficult to reveal himself *viva voce* to even his closest friends, it seemed that by writing poetry to Vittoria he was able to set his thoughts to verse as a genuine impulse of the heart. Since he kept no intimate journals throughout his lifetime, poetry allowed him to express his deepest thoughts in a way that could safely be read by another. So complex was his rhyme sometimes (as one commentator observed: 'rough, carved in stone, scarcely articulated, dark as December vespers, and yet intimate and suggestive...') that for many readers he might sound almost hermetic. The poet Aretino, a great admirer of the artist, claimed that Michelangelo often imitated the philosophers with his veiled truths.

Vittoria responded with her own sonnet, alluding to the greatness of his spirit, but at the same time making him aware of how dependent he was on God's love for him. At the same time, she confesses to him that she is his 'new mother' – a remarkable statement to make. Does this say something about their relationship? One must ask this question, as problematic as it might seem. Knowing little of Michelangelo's relationship with his mother, who is never mentioned in any of his writings, and aware of his milk-mother relationship as a child, I ask myself whether he yearned for some contact with what I will call mother-love.

Because your mind, girt and adorned well
With the eternal light, preserves of God
The likeness in that innermost abode
Where never may unfaithful image dwell.

Haply, since ardent longing doth impel,
Which never knows fulfilment but increase,
As is true lover's want, even this may please
And prove in painted form acceptable.

And thinking thus, my lord, your humble, new
Mother and handmaid sends the work to you
A better Master fashioned in your heart.

Nor be it troublesome to tell, she prays,
If this resemble that in any part
On which your high desires forever gaze.[21]

A second sonnet that she sent to Michelangelo further reinforces her desire that Michelangelo accept her devotional gifts for what they are: an affirmation of her belief that he, the greatest of artists, is beholden to God alone for the richness of his talent.

As much as human mind can apprehend
By long-time study with the guidance dear
Of heaven, whose lovely light the truth makes clear,
So much I think your noble soul has gleaned.

Wherefore, in no wise, light or strength to lend
Unto the ray of your rare steadfast faith,
That by its works to the world witnesseth
And of the other is sure pledge, I send

---

21   *Vittoria Colonna*, Maud F. Jerrold. London: J.M. Dent & Co. 1906.

> To you His image Who unto the spear
> Upon the cross His breast did offer, so
> That on your sacred blood may pour;
>
> But only, lord, because to you below
> A book more learned never opened here
> To make you live above for evermore.[22]

In this sonnet the marchioness displayed her unassuming wisdom in the way she addresses Michelangelo, her dearest friend. She becomes the wise goddess, much as he portrayed her in his drawing of Venus mentioned earlier. There we see her with steadfast gaze peering into the essence of things, a Greek goddess no less, dressed in the garb of her time. Aside from plaited hair emerging from her cowl, Michelangelo has portrayed Vittoria in the classic pose of a prophetess. He has drawn on her head the horns associated with the power of prophesy, the same horns that he carved on his sculpture of *Moses* in Pope Julius' tomb.

It is hard to convey the strange appeal these two people of such differing backgrounds exercised over one another. Were it not for poetry and religion, which they both loved, it is likely that their friendship would have descended into con-

---

22   Ibid.

ventionalities intrinsic to the period. Because Vittoria found religion so interesting, not only as a way of life but as a mode of thinking, I believe she may have found ineffable happiness in making it an important part of his. It is clear from his letters that he believed this to be so. Vittoria was his Muse, but she was also his conscience.

Ascanio Condivi, who knew Vittoria and Michelangelo well, commented about their relationship in his little book, *The Life of Michelangelo:* 'In particular he greatly loved the Marchesa di Pescara, of whose divine spirit he was enamoured, being in turn tenderly loved by her, and he had received from her several letters full of pure and most sweet love, such as would have issued from such a heart. She returned to Rome from Viterbo and other places, whither she had gone for pleasure or to spend the summer, for no other reason than to see Michelangelo...'[23] This affection is more than demonstrated by her own words to him: 'Wherefore, knowing our steadfast friendship and most sure affection bound in a Christian knot, I do not think it necessary for me to procure by my letters the testimony of yours...'[24] Michelangelo himself confessed to Condivi that, 'from

---

23   Ascanio Condivi, *The Life of Michelangelo*. London: Pallas Athene Press, 2013.
24   Ibid. Jer.

the rough model from which he was born, she had reformed and made him.'[25]

What did such a love produce that has managed to withstand the passage of time? It is a question worthy of addressing. Michelangelo and Vittoria Colonna raised their friendship above that of the normal commonplaces and monotony that beset daily life. Their relationship embodied the idea of Platonic love, something much talked about in their time, but rarely enacted. Love of friendship has its own distinct individuality, which rises above that of siblings and sets it apart from the love of husband and wife. In the case of Michelangelo, friendship did not come easy to him, given the nature of his fractious temperament. When he met Vittoria he was nothing if not a solitary old man, in many ways unfulfilled in his own life, other than as an artist. She, too, lived among ghosts of the past, and perhaps longed to reach out to a man of his unusual genius in order to diminish the emptiness that she felt in the wake of her husband's death, and of his fall from grace.

Yet there was one further gift that their friendship offered to posterity, aside from Michelangelo's remarkable poems. In the year when they first

---

25   Ibid. Con.

met, Vittoria presided over a number of meetings between the artist and other guests, as well as a visiting miniature painter from Portugal. These meetings produced three important dialogues with the artist that tell us so much about how Michelangelo viewed his role as an artist. It was Vittoria, however, who brought them all together. She alone possessed the authority to invite her good friend to St. Silvestro where she resided so that he might air his views in the presence of Francisco de Holanda, the painter from Portugal.

5

It is not often that a short text springs forth from history in a way that brings to life people that we think we know. In the case of Michelangelo we hear his voice through his letters and his poems, but most of all through his great artistic works. Yet is it his true voice? We do not hear him speaking; rather, we hear him through the thoughts of others - a Vasari or a Condivi, to name but a few. The man's complex personality is, of course, on view, and we try to understand him as best we can. We even interrogate his work in a bid to deepen our knowledge of his character. But something eludes us: we always sense that in spite of what we know about his life, he is secretly hiding from us.

Yet a little book does sometimes come along to enliven our understanding. When Francisco de Holanda presented himself in the church of San Silvestro one Sunday afternoon in Rome, there to meet Vittoria Colonna and her good friend

Michelangelo, we are at once thrown back to a time when people did come together to talk and discuss weighty subjects. The book, *Da Pintura Antiga* (publ. 1548) includes four dialogues supposedly conducted between he, Vittoria Colonna, Michelangelo, and two others. In it the voice and personality of both Vittoria and Michelangelo are heard for the first time in company. Her laughter, her wit, and his generosity of spirit, are all on show. Most of all, we learn what it is to be an artist, and what is expected of an artist, outside the general mannerism of the age.

It is important to hear their voices and what they thought about if we are to understand why they meant so much to one another. Religion, we know, meant a great deal to both of them, and they felt secure in one another's acceptance. We even know how much they enjoyed poetry as an expression of their mutual esteem. But there is another element to their friendship that is less obvious; and that is revealed in Holandia's *Dialogues*. As a young man freshly arrived in Rome at the behest of his king in Portugal, he was fortunate enough to have made the acquaintance of Vittoria Colonna, as well as Michelangelo. Though he was evidently in awe of the great man, and of the marchioness, it did not prevent him from putting down their thoughts in a way that makes them accessible to us today.

The *Dialogues* are a window into how Italians felt about art and literature during the period we know as the late Renaissance. No book gives us a better picture of the nature of the self - conscious artist, and of those who patronized the arts. This symbiosis is rare in any age; but during these years great artists and aesthetes, whether prince or pope, came together as one. All saw the value of art, whether in painting or in literature, as the glue that made the idea of culture and humanism somehow stick together. Only art made it possible for the human ideal to survive so many invasions, so much duplicity, and so little belief in Italy as being one country.

Vittoria made these Sunday afternoons possible. She invited Michelangelo to attend, so that the young Holanda might be able to ask him questions about art. It might be, too, that she had her own agenda: to hear from the lips of her great friend his thoughts on art that she had not been able to elicit from him herself. Such was the respect in which Michelangelo was held that sometimes it was difficult to allow him to speak professionally. For many people he was a man who lived in his own ivory tower, so that his opinions about art remained largely unknown.

Even friends like Vasari were unable to elicit his deepest considerations on such matters.

The marchioness was also no slouch when it came to discussing art. In the *Dialogues* we hear her defending the value of 'holy painting' with passion and with zeal. 'It brings joy in melancholy. It brings both the contented and the angry man to the knowledge of human misery,' she says. 'It moves the obstinate to compunction, the mundane to penitence, the contemplative to contemplation.'[26] Most of all, she argues, it animates and creates daring, a theme that Michelangelo later takes up in one of his conversations. Her paean to art concludes with Vittoria almost in tears when she says, 'To one who dies, it [art] gives many years of life.' It becomes clear that the role of art as a spiritual catalyst meant a great deal to people of culture in the Italy of her day.

Michelangelo, of course, places special emphasis on the God-given nature of art. To be a great master a man must be wise, and conduct himself in a measured and reasoned manner. The role of discretion was important to him too. This manifests itself in design, 'which by another name is drawing.' Drawing is at the root of all fine sculpture, painting, and architecture. To draw well is

---

26 Francisco de Holanda, *Dialogues with Michelangelo*. London: Pallas Athene, 2006.

to claim understanding of the objective world, and thus to understand the workings of God. The idea that painting was a form of 'dumb poetry' was reiterated by one of the guests at the second Dialogue meeting. To support his argument, the gentleman reminded the others of Demosthenes' remark that *writing* was called 'drawing' to the ancient Greeks, that of *'antigraphia'*.

Holanda comes to the defense of painting, if only to honour Michelangelo who is present. He says to the gentleman who has made the remark about 'dumb poetry' the following:

> Senor Lattanzio, in calling painting *dumb* poetry it seems to me that the poets did not know how to paint well, because, if they understood how much more painting declares than speaks than poetry, her sister, they would not say it was dumb, and I will maintain rather that poetry is the more dumb.[27]

Holanda in all earnestness proceeds to mount a vigorous defense of painting against the perception that poetry is the greater form of expression. He makes a powerful argument filled with classical allusions to Virgil, Homer, and others. The idea that a picture contained a better reading of reality than that of poetry is an interesting one, and Vittoria is quick to commend him with

---
27 Ibid.

her playful banter: 'You, Senor Francisco, have done so well for your inamorata [painting], that, if Maestro Michelangelo does not show just as great a sign of love for her, we may perhaps get her to divorce him and go with you to Portugal!'[28] To which Michelangelo, smilingly responds: 'He knows Madam, that I have entirely done so, and that I have already released her entirely to him; for as I do not possess such powers as such great love demands, he has said what he has said, as of one who belongs to him.' It is the mark of Michelangelo's habitual humility that cedes to the young artist everything he might have said of himself.

Holanda tells a beautiful story in defense of the power of art to transform memory. It is a story that Michelangelo, when he hears it told to those present that day, readily concurs. Moreover, it is one that has all the hallmarks of the late medieval sense of the objectness of things, as distinct to a truly imaginative engagement with reality:

> But I cannot omit to mention a painting that I saw, even though it was outside Italy... in the city of Avignon...: it is that of a dead woman who had been very beautiful, called the Beautiful Anna. A king of France, who very much enjoyed painting, and painted himself (whose name, I believe, was

28   Ibid.

Reynel) visited Avignon to inquire whether the Beautiful Anna was there, as he wished to see her and paint her from life. He was told that she had died shortly before. The king ordered her to be disinterred in order that he might see in her bones whether there were some traces of her beauty left. He found her fully clothed in the old style, as if she were alive, with her golden hair dressed on her head, but all the gay beauty of her face, which alone was uncovered, had changed into a skull. Notwithstanding his disappointment, the king considered it so beautiful that he painted her from nature, surrounding his portrait with verses which mourn and still mourn for her.[29]

The idea that art can transform reality is at the heart of this remarkable story. Michelangelo, who was a close observer of nature, at least when it pertained to the human body (he spent a good deal of time in mortuaries sketching corpses, though much to his distaste), understood how an artist might wish to take reality and then transform it into an object of beauty. The story that the young Holanda told them was a perfect example of the Platonism which Michelangelo so readily espoused in his own work. He wanted to make the 'ordinary body' into an object of transcendence.

---

29 Ibid. Note: The king mentioned in the story was said to be Rene the Good of Anjou (1409-80), King of Naples and Aragon: the painting of 'La Bella Anna' attributed to him is now lost.

Though Michelangelo did not talk much about his own art during these discussions, Vittoria was never one to allow those present to forget that he was, after all, the master. We sense her desire to serve her friend as the loyal acolyte of his genius. It was this quality, I suspect, that endeared her most to Michelangelo. He hated fawning admiration; but when the marchioness spoke, and spoke with knowledge at her fingertips, he accepted her compliments with good grace. For her, his artistry was the embodiment of the man. It echoed her own poetic sensibility, forged as it had been on the anvil of suffering and disappointment, that she knew he had experienced also. Like him, art served as a memorial of the present for those who came after.

Michelangelo does hold strong opinions about art, however, and can be inveigled into discussing them if Vittoria so chooses to draw him out. 'I beg of your Excellency to tell me,' he says, 'what I can give to her and it shall be hers.' And she, smiling, replies: 'I very much wish to know what you think of the painting of Flanders, and whether it is more devout than the Italian style.' To which Michelangelo responds with a detailed examination of the flaws and failures of Flemish art. 'It tries to do too many things at once, so that it does not do anything really well.' The master has spoken; only Italian art reigns supreme in that it has the capacity to unite itself with God, and so copy the perfections of God. Finally, he says: 'Good painting is music and melody which the intellect only can appreciate, and then with great difficulty... Since art belongs to no country, but *comes from heaven,* and even thought from ancient times it has remained in Italy more than any other kingdom in the world, I think it will be the end of it.' Holanda concludes his exposition with these words: 'So he spoke. Michelangelo was now silent.' Such a pronouncement seems almost biblical, but it does indicated the veneration in which Michelangelo was held by those present that day.[30]

We find so many interesting ideas about art coming from the lips of those present in San Silvestro over succeeding Sundays. All knew the complexities of art as practice, and they understood its relationship with the other arts such as poetry. 'Good painting as melody', 'painting as dumb poetry', these are interesting observations, and suggest how important it was in the sixteenth-century to analyze the essence of art, and not just to do it. Moreover, there was this sense that art did more than provide decoration in palazzo or garden: it informed all science, all

---

30   Ibid.

practical activities such as architecture, coinage, sculpture, fortifications and armour, as well as the crafts. It was the binding agent of all human activity – more so than trade or mercantilism. Men like Michelangelo saw themselves as men of science as much as they were artists.

In response to a question put to him by Diego Zapata, one of those present during the third dialogue, where the gentleman asks him why artists paint so many monsters and beasts with the faces of women, or anthropomorphic beings with legs and the tails of fishes – in short, 'painting which delights the painters, and which is never seen in the world' – Michelangelo responds accordingly: 'Poets and painters have the power to dare, I mean to dare and do whatever they may approve of.' In this remark we hear the full force of Michelangelo's personality as an artist. He has spent his lifetime daring to complete the impossible. Whether it is his *David* or his half-carved *Fettered Slaves* emerging from marble, we are made aware of the sheer force of his energy as an artist being brought to bear. He is never satisfied with mere illustration, or copying. Michelangelo wants to *create* what is not there, a 'monster' capable of delighting all our sensibilities.

Indeed, in many of his poems, particularly in those dedicated to Vittoria, Michelangelo does analyze his relationship to his art practice. It is clear that the act of daring is central to his belief in the power of art to change how we view the world. I am not aware of any artist before Michelangelo to be so specific about the need to risk everything in the realization of beauty. Did he acquire this understanding from his religious belief (Christ as hero, Christ as martyr), and was it refined as a concept in his discussions with Vittoria? We shall never know. His poetry, however, gives us ample opportunity to meditate upon the link between beauty as an objective reality and its relationship with the divine.

> From birth I was granted beauty
> To be my vocation's faithful guide;
> Mirror and light is it for me
> In both the arts. He who thinks
> Otherwise is mistaken. My eye
> Ascends to those heights where
> I sit down to paint and sculpt.
>
> If those of rash and stupid opinion
> Drag beauty down to the senses
> Though every healthy mind
> Is borne by it to heaven, let them
> Know that an infirm eye does not
> Move from the mortal to the divine
> Sphere, but remains forever
> Fixed there, where any thought
> Of rising without grace is a vain hope.

And, in a later sonnet (see XXI) we hear how the divine works through the material, whether it is marble or by way of the brush itself. For Michelangelo, a true artist operates in collusion with God, an idea that we find in Plato and his theory of the Good, and of his primordial Ideas:

> If the divine part of an artist observes
> Someone's face and gestures through
> A multiple power and gives life to stone,
> This isn't the result of mere craft.
>
> It operates in the roughest design, before
> A steady hand raises a brush, as the divine
> Part experiments on the most interesting
> Of ideas, thus arranging perfect figures.

Another important concept that Michelangelo alluded to in his conversations about art was that of *sprezzatura*. It is a word that finds its origin in Castiligione's *Courtier*, where he speaks of an apparent effortlessness required to conceal the difficulty of bringing a work of art to fruition. Michelangelo alludes to *sprezzatura* when he replies to remarks made by Holanda about perfection in art.

> And I wish to tell you, Francisco de Holanda, of an exceedingly great beauty in this science of ours, and which I think you consider the highest, namely that what one has most to work and struggle for in painting is to do the work with a great amount of labour and sweat in such a way that it may afterwards appear, however much it was labored, to have been done almost quickly and almost with-

out labour, and very easily, although it is not. And this is a very excellent beauty…[31]

Such is the nature of Michelangelo's artistry. It is a quality, I believe, that he brought to bear upon his relationship with Vittoria Colonna. The two of them engaged in an act of *sprezzatura* throughout the years that they knew one another. They found a way to be effortless in one another's presence, in spite of their many differences – in age, in class and background, in their understanding of the duties of love. The wonder of it is that they managed to surmount their own fraught pasts as lovers and wives. Holanda's little book of *Dialogues* captures the spirit of *sprezzatura* between Michelangelo and Vittoria Colonna perfectly.

We are left with a sense that Michelangelo and Vittoria enjoyed one another's company, both socially, as well as intellectually. They embodied, too, the very essence of the humanist ideal in the late sixteenth-century. Like many of their counterparts they believed in a spirit of order and beauty in knowledge, and how to convey that enthusiasm to themselves. This was a moment when the world seemed so vital, when a new type of mythology was being born. As Pico wrote

---

31 Ibid.

to Politiziano, his friend, 'Love God, we rather may, than either know Him, or utter Him. And yet had men lived by knowledge do never find that which they seek, which also without love were in vain found.' It may be that Vittoria and Michelangelo, in spite of what they knew themselves, found that love Pico speaks of through their mutual love of God.

Holanda's *Dialogues* offer us a unique insight into their relationship. I begin to see them as two people in collusion. She who struggled with her past and her religious concerns; he with his complexities as an emotionally immature man in league with his art. They felt a need to reach out and help one another in their plight. It is not such an unusual expectation: friendship, indeed love, is wedded to such a need. Where theirs stand apart from other relationships, I believe, is in the realization of a body of extraordinary love poems. The sixteenth-century had not seen such an impassioned belief in the power of love to heal the soul. Not only was Michelangelo an artistic titan, it seems, but he was also a great poet.

6

Michelangelo's belief that his destiny was determined by his formative years living in the quarries of Settignano while under the care of a wet-nurse says a good deal about his almost totemistic feeling for stone. He possessed an inordinate feeling for what he called 'hard, alpine marble', and how, cutting into it was an act of *forze di lavare*, the power to extract something beautiful out of a formless piece of rock. The years he spent in Carrara wandering about its quarries, too, suggest a man who preferred the dust-grimed life of a stone cutter to that of an artist. It is not quite true, of course; but we must accept that his love of marble coincided with his isolation as a human being.

His poetry also bears the marks of an object carved from stone. Dense, elliptic, fragmentary and broken sometimes, it bears little resemblance to the elegant verses of Dante or Petrarch, both of whom he greatly admired. It is said that Michelangelo knew more than any man in Florence the verses of *La Vita Nuova* and the *Commedia*. When he was in Bologna as a guest of a nobleman there, he used to read aloud in Tuscan accents to his host from Dante and Petrarch until the man went to sleep, thus paying for his keep. Though he cribbed from their work often enough, his style was such that both poets became lost in translation. Fire and ice became the leitmotif of his images, along with chisel and mallet. With these he could 'conquer nature' and make a work of art from it that might defeat time and death.

Stone was the material from which he carved forms, but words were the primary material of his thoughts. When, in later life, he attempted to express his love for Vittoria Colonna two years before her death, he found it impossible sometimes to untangle his words from his art as a sculptor. Only in words, however, could he understand his motives: when he carved stone he was carving himself. To understand Michelangelo as a poet, one must accept this confusion. Perhaps Vittoria was the only person who could do so. Though he might draw her occasionally, and write many poems to her, he could never bring himself to sculpt or paint the marchioness. It was as if she must remain forever absent from her physical presence, a wraithlike odalisque in the mind of the artist.

> When an artist chisels in hard stone
> He sometimes renders that person
> Like himself. And if I carve a woman's
> Face bleak and sad, it is my features
> I model because she has made me so;
> The stone's harshness resembles her
> Because I am simply unable to sculpt
> Anything other than my pain-filled face
> When she so spurns and despises me.
> Through the ages art records beauty;
> If her wish is to endure, then let her
> Make me forever happy, so that I
> Might make her eternally beautiful.
> (XXXVI)

It may be, of course, that he was afraid of enlivening Vittoria as a work of art. Her meaning in his life could not be sculpted because he feared the consequences – that his own longing for death might be imposed upon a woman that he loved. As he wrote in one of his early madrigals, 'Where death is, Love will not approach.' Moreover, when she did pass away in 1547, seventeen years before he did, he was utterly devastated. She had not cheated death, while he was condemned to live on, an old man, knowing that his memory of her was never sharpened by any painting of his.

> Each time appears my lady's face
> Before my heart's eye, whether
> Weak or strong, death arranges itself

> Between these opposing images, yet
> Terrifies me more when it drives
> Away that muddled facade.
>
> (XXXVII)

It is hard to approach Michelangelo's poetry as a literary critic, such is its *spessezza* or density. One looks into his verses much as if they were lava bubbling inside a volcano. They pulsate, they plop and conflate before one has time to find their meaning. Each words jags against the next, never smoothly or elegantly, but in a way that heralds some kind of enormous pressure acting upon Michelangelo's thoughts. Such words as 'destroys and despises me' *(mi strugge e sprezza)* remind us of the blow of mallet on chisel. Michelangelo is attacking marble when he tries to fashion a poem out of nothing. He knows the poems is imbedded in his mind somewhere, just as he knows that a figure is imbedded in a block of stone.

Clearly, he is never far from his craft when he composes his verses to Vittoria. One imagines him at night in his house in Rome, still covered in dust from his work on those monumental statues destined for the Tomb of Julius (he rarely washed), and remembering how he had fashioned Moses as a prophet perhaps, finally picking up a pen to compose. His square forehead and flattened nose capture the light from a candle.

His hand does not shake, such is his strength. The extreme tension with which he imbues his sculptures and paintings, that boundless energy which animates all his figures, these are also present in his poetry. We are aroused by his ability to convey an infinity of spirit, whether it is in his plastic artistry or in his poems. In them both he strains at the limits, without ever quite breaking them.

How did Vittoria Colonna react to Michelangelo's poems when they were delivered to her in the monastery? We have so few of her letters addressed to him, so it is hard to form any opinion. But one does have the sense that his poems meant a lot to her. She particularly admired his wholehearted dedication to his art, something that few artists of his time attempted to copy. Michelangelo placed himself above the Maecenate system of patronage that largely determined how an artist engaged with the art patrons of his time. He even took pride in not removing an old felt hat from his head in the presence of a pope! Unlike men such as Bramante and Raphael, he did not ingratiate himself with the Vatican. He actually quit Rome on one occasion because of a slight by one pope who chose to treat him as a mere employee.

We therefore must assume that Michelangelo found a sympathetic response from the marchioness, one that encouraged him to write the many poems that we find in this book. She made it possible for him to express his deep piety, knowing that she was wedded to the idea of spiritual renewal in the Church of Rome, and therefore not immune to his craggy sensibility with regard to the suffering that he experienced in his later years. There is never any sense that Michelangelo reached a plateau of calm in his life. Nor that he was ever reconciled to the lack of love that he felt was his lot.

At the same time, his poetry is tinged with the old troubadour tradition of *fin' amors,* the medieval belief of love as an act of courtesy. The central tenet of *fin' amors* prescribed that a man must be at the service of the woman he chooses to adore. It also required the renunciation of the immediate, close, and deceitful love that characterized normal relations between men and women. Sensual love was thus overcome by reason. Fidelity was at the heart of such a relationship. The woman must remain forever inaccessible, and conform to a Platonic type. The profane ideal of happiness governed by the senses was thus transformed into a more refined form of love dominated by the imagination.

It was this kind of love that both Michelangelo and Vittoria Colonna agreed to respect, even if they did not mention it as their ideal. Many of Michelangelo's poems reflect his desire to place Vittoria on a pedestal, and not to allow venality to enter their dealings with one another. This is the classic ploy of the troubadour poet: to mask his affections by creating an idealized view of love itself. Time and again Michelangelo resorted to this ploy in his poems. He had found a way to replicate the idealism of his great mentor, Dante, who employed this same method in *La Vita Nuova*. It might be worthwhile to make a comparison between Michelangelo and Dante in this respect.

> It may be true that something beautiful
> Raises perfect desire from the world
> To God through the intercession
> Of my lady, whose eyes have been formed
> In its image, as have mine. All else I forget
> Caring for her alone. No greater wonder is it
> If I love and long for her, and call out
> To her all the time; nor am I worthy
> If by its very nature, my soul comes to rest
> On she whose eyes resemble those eyes
> From which it emerged. If my soul accepts
> Love first as its apogee, then it honours
> Her here and now for that end's sake:
> Whoever adores his lord love his servant.
>
> (V)

Dante, on hearing of the death of Beatrice, finds himself addressing her memory as his *fin' amors* in a similar fashion in *La vita Nuova*:

> Beyond the broad, encircling spheres
> A sigh that quits my heart aspires to move.
> A new celestial effect that Love bestows
> By virtue of his unceasing tears
> Impels it upward. As it nears its goal
> Of longing in the realms above
> The pilgrim spirit sees a vision of
> A soul in glory whom the host reveres.
> Gazing at her, it speaks of what it sees
> In words so subtle I do not understand
> Within my sad heart which bids it tell.
> That noble one is named, as I apprehend
> For frequently it mentions the name Beatrice
> This much, beloved ladies, I know well.

It is likely that the artist was familiar with the work of Italian troubadours such as Ferrari da Ferrara who compiled a florilegium of troubadour poets in the Occitan language in the 13-14th century. Sordello, too, was well known to him through his reading of Dante, who placed the poet in Purgatory for his pains. While many of his poems addressed to Vittoria appear to be confessional, they also partake of that astringency we find in the work of other poets, such as the famous *trobar clus* poet Marcebru of southwest France.[32] So that while Michelangelo might allude to his respect for the work of Petrarch, it is clear that he was influenced by a broad range of poets, many of them subliminally. We know that he paid close attention to technique, and matured as a poet over the period of his long life.

Another poet who may well have influenced Michelangelo was Guido Guinizelli (1230-76), the founder of the 'sweet new style' (*Dolce stil novo*) made famous by Dante himself. He, like Michelangelo, tried to reconcile divine and earthy love, along with the depiction of deep psychological introspection. Even as the spirit of God is poured from heaven to move us, so does the noble face of a woman move us. In Michelangelo's madrigal (III) we hear echoes of this same sentiment:

> It's impossible that her holy eyes
> Should draw delight from mine
> Since to her divine gaze I offer
> No more than sad and bitter tears
> In return for her sweet smiles.

---

32   Marcebru (fl. 1130-50) was the patron of the *trobar clus* style or 'closed' style of writing. It entailed the interweaving within a poem of more than one level of meaning within a poem, and the gradual revealing, to the observant listener, of a hidden treasure lying below the surface.

The holy eyes of the beloved become a reflection of God on earth, just as it does for Guinizelli:

> I never used to think that my heart
> Could have such tormented thoughts
> That my tearful soul might be born
> Revealing a face with dead eyes.
>
> I felt neither peace nor rest
> In the place where I found love
> And my Lady, who said to me
> You won't escape, my strength's greater.

This is not to say that he did not hear the voices of his contemporaries, men such as Aretino and Ariosto. Their poetry, however, is largely epic or satiric in tone, which had little impact upon Michelangelo's work. In any event, he had no love for Aretino after the man had disparaged him by publicly denouncing his liking for young men. In the *Last Judgment*, Michelangelo painted the poet as St Bartholomew, the saint who was skinned alive at the time of his crucifixion. He depicted him holding up the flayed pelt of the artist himself. It was Michelangelo's angry response to a self-confessed sodomite, and an ex-friend. He remained true to the sonnet and the madrigal for the most part, however, and only rarely ventured into the longer, ballad form, which did not really suit the intensity of his thought. With his lack of a clear vision of nature in any of his works also, bucolic poetry was equally outside his preserve. Strangely enough, only three trees grace his entire painterly oeuvre. He was no *paysagiste*, not at all!

Michelangelo was left alone to eke out the remaining years of his life without his beloved Vittoria. We cannot begin to know how he felt not having her to turn to. The last poems written in the late 1550s chart his increasing need to address God, rather than someone else. With Vittoria's departure there was no one he could truly reach out to for succour. In one sonnet sent to his scholar friend, Ludovico Beccadelli, we hear him grappling with his own failed illusions and need to rise above them.

> This world's illusions have stolen from me
> The time I needed to contemplate God;
> Not only have I discarded His graces, sin has
> Claimed me more fully than if I'd lacked them.
>
> What makes others blind makes me blind
> And foolish, slow to see the error of my ways;
> Hope fades, even as my desire increases, that
> By you I might be free of selfish love.
>
> My dear Lord, shorten the road that leads
> To heaven, and help me to climb
> What little of the path is left open to me.
>
> Cause me to hate all that the world values
> All its beauties I so love and revere, that
> Before death I might receive eternal life.

In the end, renunciation becomes one of the most persistent themes of his later poetry. I believe he had received this insight from Vittoria herself. Even at the time when he first met her she had long since abnegated her role as a public figure, and retired into a semi-monastic life. There had been two Vittoria Colonnas, it seems, one of high pomp and another of keen abstinence. We catch a glimpse of the former at the wedding of the King of Poland and Isabella of Aragona in Naples one year.

> Next came the most illustrious Marchesa di Pescara, mounted on a black and white steed, whose trappings were of crimson velvet, with a fringe of gold and silver. Around her were six grooms, dressed in doublets and jerkins of blue and yellow satin. She wore a petticoat of brocade of dark red velvet, with large splays of beaten gold... On her head she wore a coif of gold, and in her train were six waiting-women, attired in blue damask.[33]

To which another observer offers a later version of the same woman:

> It was already the seventh year since the Marchese of Pescara had ascended to a better life, when Vittoria, having vainly made trial by effort to free her soul from sadness and sorrow, recognized but too clearly the misery of those who live according to

---

33 *Vittoria Colonna*, Alethea B. Weil. London 1889.

> the appetites of nature; and the goods of this earth resemble the rose, where thorns are inseparably joined to it, therefore she disposed herself to the raising of her mind, and fixed them on divine ones...[34]

Michelangelo knew only the woman who had adopted the spiritual life, and who had fixed her thoughts on heavenly things, not the one who rode in sumptuous carriages. This woman helped him to feel at ease with himself, in spite of his perennial conflicts. She had opened the way for him to express his own love of God, and his own need to free himself from the ordinary venalities of his daily life. We will never see Michelangelo rise to the level of acceptance that Vittoria was able to achieve; this was not his destiny. He was a man imbued with a powerful creative energy that could not be tamed by asceticism or by resignation.

He was his own David, one-eyed, a man fascinated by Cyclopean giants. Nothing was small in his world. No artist before him had graced his time with such magnificent obsessions, either. He could paint or sculpt only God-like themes at the expense of all else. Nor did he have any interest in the goings-on of ordi-

---

34   Ibid.

nary mortals, for whom he held little regard. Like Dante before him, whom he wished to emulate, he wanted to capture the human spirit as an embodiment of ever gesture of the bodily frame itself. For him, the male torso was the ultimate expression of masculinity, the very essence of man's triumph over the will. Only one person could hold him to account for his obsession with such masculinity, however, and that was Vittora Colonna. In her own way she imbued him with the sensibilities of a fawn. The wavering flame that shone brightly in his soul could not be pacified by the wind, but only by a lady who understood how to shield such agitation with her sympathy, her calmness, and the grace of her person. He had met his match.

7

It is true: Michelangelo's obsession with giants and one-eyed people in his poetry tells a lot about his struggle with power and insight as the ruling motifs of his work as an artist. It is no accident that one of his greatest works of sculpture should be David who defeats Goliath, the giant. And that he should write a long poem celebrating the dubious merits of a giant. Normally it is regarded as a medical condition; and yet in Michelangelo's case, he clearly saw gigantism as a reflection of his will to power. As his star rose, and his reputation soared, he obviously felt threatened by his own titanic nature. Such is his genius, however, that he was able to resort to what he believed was his greatest asset: a clear eye. 'Love gave me a clear eye,' he wrote in one of his early poems, which he later elaborated upon in a sonnet written for Vittoria. There he pleaded with her to 'make of his body a single eye'.[35]

The death of Vittoria came as a shock to Michelangelo, who surely expected to die before his beloved friend. Illness had forced her to be removed from her convent to the Cesarini Palace in central Rome. On 15th February 1527 the marchioness made her will, requesting that her brother Ascanio Colonna be appointed her principal heir. Ten days later she breathed her last, with Michelangelo by her side. This moment is surely one of the most poignant in the often turbulent lives of these two remarkable people. The greatest artist of his age seated beside one of its finest poets, religious reformers, and spiritual intellects: the rough hands of an elderly sculptor holding those of a woman whose cultivated persona was legendary, such were their lives intermingled in the name of posterity.

Condivi tells us that after her death Michelangelo remained for a long time bereft of all sense, walking about in a dazed state. At the last, and on her request, he had drawn a picture of the *Deposition of Christ,* with the dead Son fallen at the feet of his mother, the Virgin Mary, who stares towards heaven with her hands outstretched. On

---

35   See Sonnet XXVI.

the stem of the cross Michelangelo had written *Non vi si pensa quanto sangue costa!* ('little one knows how much His blood has cost'). It was his way of saying that together they had fashioned a love for one another which had transcended time and circumstance. His one regret, he confessed, was that he had only kissed her hand at death and not her face or brow. In the end, it seems, discretion and an all-consuming respect for his friend had prevented him from doing so. She was, in many respects, his Virgin Mother.

His own death, which he always thought was imminent, did not occur until many years later. It appears that man who had once been a sickly child had outlasted all his contemporaries, including his younger brothers. Living on amid failing health and loneliness, he somehow managed to pen sonnets that reflected his growing awareness of the spiritual life for the benefit of his few friends. He has, however, left to us his final impressions of Vittoria in two moving sonnets (XXXXIII and XXXXIV), the last ones that he dedicated to her memory. In one of them he writes:

> In one short breath, an instant! God has gathered
> Her body back unto Himself from a world
> Unaware of it, and removed it from our eyes.
> (XXXXIII)

Such are the lines of a man who understood how contingent we all are in this life, thus mirroring those written by his great mentor, Dante, in *Paradiso:*

> Contingence, which does exercise no right
> Beyond that frame of matter where you lie,
> Stands all depicted in the Eternal Sight.[36]

After Vittoria's death Michelangelo chose to spend most of his time meditating upon the thought of death in the hope of resisting what he called the 'vain distractions of love' that might have preoccupied him in the past. 'I may remind you that a man,' he wrote, 'who would fain return unto and enjoy his own self ought not to indulge so much in merrymakings and festivities, but to think upon death. This thought is the only one which makes us know our proper selves... Marvelous is the operation of this thought of death... which defends all of us from human passions.'[37] Self-control, and an understanding of God, had become his ruling passions.

In pain, brought low by gallstone problems and other ailments, the old man began to per-

---

36 Dante, *Il Paradiso,* Canto XVII, 1.37-39. Transl. Dorothy L. Sayers. London: Penguin Books, 1971

37 See Guasti, *Rime,* p.31.

ceive that his end was near. 'The end may not be just now, but I fear greatly that it cannot be far off,' he wrote. On 14th February 1564 he retired to his easy chair beside the fire and slowly slipped into slumber. He expressed a desire to ride one more time during one of his waking moments, as was his daily regimen, but that was no longer possible. On 18th February he suffered what is likely to have been a heart attack, and died at 5pm that day, surrounded by his physicians, a few months before his ninetieth birthday. Vasari tells us that during his last moments he muttered his last will and testimony 'in three sentences', committing his soul into the hands of God, his body to the earth, and his goods to his nearest relatives. Thus the greatest of all artists passed away. It is said, though how reliable the information is, that his last act was to caress the marble fragment of the Belvedere Torso which he had used as a study in many of his fresco figures.[38] Ever the sculptor, it seems, Michelangelo want-

---

38 The Belvedere Torso is a marble fragment of a nude male statue, signed prominently on the front of the base by 'Apollonios, son of Nestor, Athenian.' According to the Vatican Museum the most favoured hypothesis identifies it with Ajax, the son of Telamon, in the act of contemplating his suicide. How it might have come into Michelangelo's possession is unknown. We see the Torso replicated in the Sistine Chapel as St Bartolommeo, and a caricature of Aretino. The Torso gained the sobriquet, 'The School of Michelangelo.'

ed to feel his beloved marble under his fingertips one last time. Carrera was in his bones.

His death signaled the end of the period that we know of as the High Renaissance. Born into and a part of its enthusiasms, along with such great artists as Piero della Francesca, Leonardo da Vinci, Rafael, Titian, and Botticelli, he was its living embodiment. The sheer variety of his oeuvre overshadows all other artists of his time. Emerging from the circle of Lorenzo like an eagle from its eyrie, he bestowed his concept of beauty upon everything he touched. All the great ideas circulating in his time, from Plato to Plotinus, from Ficino to Mirandola, were imbued into his work. Moreover, the power of an idea was tantamount to his belief in the way he expressed himself. Of course it led to a great deal of personal self-doubt, but that was largely determined by his yearning for love throughout his life, not his understanding of the worthiness of his art.

As a poet he will always remain cloaked in obscurity. Not because he was an ordinary poet, but because he was such a great artist. In truth he was a poet of unusual sensitivity and a remarkable technique. No one before him had used his 'other craft' to inform the way he fashioned words into poetry. We sense marble dust in his every line.

We note the chisel colliding with concepts and images whenever he tried to chart the course of his thoughts. Who else but he could link one of his tools to a condition of the heart: 'Weak soul, what rough file tears/at your hide, and wears it away?'[39] That he saw himself as a flayed hide or boar's coif tells us of the almost animaline fury buried in his psyche. He was never angry with the world so much as with his inability to perfect his art. He knew, better than anyone, that mastery can only be attained at the very end of one's life.[40]

Fashioning enduring human relationships he found more difficult to achieve, however. It is for this reason that his love for Vittoria Colonna must be seen as his most successful attempt to do so. He needed such a love because it affirmed his shaky hold on normal reality. All his failed loves, all his frustrations with patrons, all his artistic difficulties with marble and pigments, these were somehow ameliorated by Vittoria's concern for him, for his well being. She made him believe that his soul was indeed worth saving, in spite of all his confessed 'sins' that we see acknowledged in his poetry. Vittoria made him feel worthy of

39 Sonnet XXI.
40 Sonnet II.

God's love in the hope of achieving a better life after death.

It is hard for us today to recognize the validity of such an imperative, given that the idea of Hell has lost its significance. Strangely enough, Michelangelo rarely, if ever, mentions it as an alternative to Heaven. What strikes us most about his poetry is his desire to *return* to God, perhaps sensing that his soul has enjoyed knowledge and love of God before the advent of his earthly life. Neo-Platonism and the lure of beauty were forever intertwined in his mind, ever since his younger days spent in the company of Marsilio Ficino and his circle of friends. His time on earth was but a pilgrimage that he must endure, and endure it he did. His work as an artist reflects all that he suffered, and all that he achieved.

Like Vittoria Colonna, his great love, Michelangelo was buried simply, outside the normal pomp of the moment.[41] He lived austerely, without any attachment to things; just as Vitto-

---

41 When his coffin passed along the streets of Florence to its final resting place in St Croce Church in the early ours of the morning, a large crowd assembled along the route to pay their respects to their greatest son. Men vied with one another to carry his coffin into the church. It was noted that when the coffin was opened twenty-five days after his death, his body was found to be perfect in all its parts. 'The head and cheeks, to the touch, felt just as though he had breathed his last but a few hours since.' (Vasari 12.290)

ria pleaded that she might be buried in common ground in the Church of St Anna, wearing the habit of a simple nun, in a 'pitched coffin' placed in a velvet case. No doubt, in the ensuing years, Michelangelo would have gone to this church to pay his respects to her memory. He would have recalled the poetry he had written to her, the letters that they exchanged, and the relief he had experienced whenever she acknowledged him with the generosity of her spirit. Their love for one another was touched by an altogether unique premise: that two people, buffeted by extreme circumstances and events, can find a way back to the depths of their mutual humanity through the love of art, of poetry, and the love of God.

Love Poems of Michelangelo

For Vittoria Colonna

I

Truly, my lady, though divine in beauty
You act like any mortal being, eating
Sleeping, and talking among us, not
To follow you when grace and mercy
Removes all doubt – what punishment
Should fit such a crime? Anyone
Who relies on his own thoughts, thus
Casting a bind eye, is slower to love
By his own effort. In me, form a shape
Fashion the outside, as I do in stone
Or on a blank sheet of parchment
Where nothing is so contained,
This embodies all that I truly wish.

II

After many years and many attempts
A true artist soon realizes a bright idea
As a living image in stone, hard and white
When he is near to death: coming late
To carving what is new and original
He remains there but a short while.
So too with nature: the height of beauty
It attains through your divine face
Is as trial and error across time, one image
Upon another, until worn away. And so

Fear, bound to beauty, feeds upon
My desire for strange flavours; nor do
I know whether the vision of your face
So beautiful, harms me more than
World's end, or gives greater delight.

III

It's impossible that her holy eyes
Should draw delight from mine
Since to her divine gaze I offer
No more than sad and bitter tears
In return for her sweet smiles.
Such is the vain hope of lovers!
How can her infinite beauty, her
Fulsome light, be so unlike mine
Far surpassing my whole self, so that
When they burn me they do not burn
Themselves? Between faces so different
And contrary, Love grows angry with me
And lamely limps away, sorrowful
That to enter her noble heart he does so
As fire, while leaving me as water.

IV

Wiles, charms, caresses, gold, feasts
And pearls: who could distinguish
What emerges from human effort
In her divine actions, when even
The silver and gold she wears
Receive their light from her, and
Doubles it? Light shining in every
Precious gem owes more to her eyes
Than to its own luminous virtue.

V

As your fury grows, my love, I'm not able
Nor do I wish to hold myself back
From saying to you, and swearing:
However harsh or indifferent you are
The more you guide and spur my soul
To virtue. If sometimes you pity
My death, and my anguished laments
As of one who is dying, I feel my heart
Slowly break within me as my torments
Grow weaker. From your bright and
Holy eyes what meager grace I've
Received is dear and sweet to me:
he who gains much by losing, learns.

VI

It may be true that something beautiful
Raises perfect desire from the world
To God through the intercession
Of my lady, whose eyes have been formed
In its image, as have mine. All else I forget
Caring for her alone. No greater wonder is it
If I love and long for her, and call out
To her all the time; nor am I worthy
If by its very nature, my soul comes to rest
On she whose eyes resemble those eyes
From which it emerged. If my soul accepts
Love first as its apogee, then it honors
Her here and now for that end's sake:
Whoever adores his lord love his servant.

VII

Now must certainly be the time
To withdraw from torment, as
Desire is not appropriate to my age.
As you well know, dear love, my soul

Is blind to the passing of time
And to the act of dying; yet even
As I face death I beg this of you –
If you have to break and shatter
Your bow into a thousand pieces,
You do not spare it any misfortune,
For a man never dies who never
Ceases to suffer constant torment.

VIII

Beautiful can you not be, nor unmerciful;
Yet being entirely mine you can't help
but destroy and consume all of me.
Since then your mercy always endures
So long as your beauty and the finality
Of your graceful face puts and end
To by burning heart. Just as the spirit
Returns to its star when set free, there
To delight He who restores bodily form
To all who die, whether in quiet peace
Or in torment that remains eternal,
So do I pray that my body, as ugly
As it is, which you attend to now, that
You will care for in paradise: a devoted
Heart is as worthy as any beautiful face.

IX

If fire burns everything, but doesn't
Consume me, it's not a sign of any great
Or lesser power at work in me, but my
Capacity to seek safety like a salamander
While others die alone. Nor do I know
What drew me from my peaceful state
To know such torment: you didn't
Create your face nor I my heart, nor shall
We ever undo the bonds of mutual love –
A higher power is He than both of us

Who has placed my life in the depths
Of your eyes. If I confess my great love
For you, and you remain untroubled
Forgive me, for I perform that suffering
Whose sole aim is my death, though it's
Not the desire of the one who kills me.

X

Less graciousness, my lady, would keep
Me alive and in rude health, my breast
Less bathed by tears from both eyes.
Redoubled pity overcomes my weakened
Powers, darkens and destroys them.
No man of wisdom wishes for more than
A jot of joy beyond his measure, but
Enough, at least, to spur him forth.
Too much joy is vain and foolish;
For a modest person tranquil peace
Is his unassuming lot. Good lady, what
Power lies within your grasp brings
Distress to me: she who gives herself
To another beyond his expectation may
Well advance death from unbridled pleasure.

XI

Lacking wit and skill as I do in the wake
Of one who steels away my life with an
Offer so excessive that I should acquire
Far more from any gift of little compassion,
Like an eye blinded by what shines too brightly
My soul takes its leave, rising above me
To a place I can't ever reach; though it doesn't
Allow me to receive the least gift from
A lady so lofty and serene. Know that it is
My incapacity which makes me feel
Ungrateful in her presence. This lady
Full of grace, spreads her gifts so lavishly

That they inflame others with such a fire
Whose excess burns with far less heat
Than what little is left over of its ardor.

XII

Great grace, dear lady, like great suffering
Can kill a thief being led away to his death
Devoid of hope and utterly paralyzed
If a pardon is suddenly presented to him.

Likewise, if your mercy, most generously
Bestowed on this misery of mine, so full
Of sorrow, and with excessive passion brings me
Peace, then will it deprive me of tears and life.

This occurs when we receive harsh or sweet news:
Though contrary, both result in instant death
Because the heart expands or contracts to much.

Your beauty, nourished by Love and heaven
Must restrain happiness if I'm to live, for a
Lesser power dies when touched by great gifts.

XIII

The greatest artist never knows what excess
Is buried in a single piece of marble,
Only a hand obeying the directions of
Intellect can discover what it contains.

The evil I flee, and the good to which I aspire
My gracious, noble, and divine lady, lies hidden
In you in the same way. If I should die, my art
Will create the opposite of what I desire.

Not Love nor your beauty, harshness or luck
Nor haughty disdain, should ever be blamed
For my sins, nor my destiny or my fate,

Unless in your heart you carry death and mercy
As well as my trivial mind - that, as it burns, isn't
Able to extract from it anything but death.

XIV

Just as, lady, by chipping away, I bring forth
A living figure from hard alpine marble
That grows larger when stone is reduced,
So do the excesses in my own flesh, with its
Course, rough, and hard skin, hide some good
In my soul, trembling under this burden.
Only you can release from my innermost being
Such a translucent and commanding figure,
For I have neither the will nor the strength.

XV

Not so unique, this mold emptied now of its
Sculpted figure, standing ready to be filled with
Either gold or silver melted over a fire, so that
A work of art is revealed when broken; I, too
Replenish the desire within me through the fireOf
love, emptied of infinite beauty by she
Whom I adore, soul and heart of my fragile life.
To be brought forth, this noble and dear lady
Is poured into me through tiny holes, so that
I too might finally be broken and shattered.

XVI

High above myself, my lady, you make
Me rise, so that speech and thought fail me
And I'm no longer myself. Why, then
If you grant me wings, do I not ascend
And fly to your lovely face? And why
Can I not stay with you if heaven has

Granted us the right to enter paradise
In the cloak of our mortal bodies?
My good fortune, I do now realize
because of your grace, allows me
to separate from my soul, so that
It alone, being so close to you, should
Escape its rendezvous with death.

XVII

No one, dear lady, may reach your high
Shining crown simply by climbing a long
Steep road, unless you reach down
With humility and kindness: the ascent
Only steepens and my strength fails, just as
My breath fails me half way along the road.
That your beauty should be so exalted
Brings deep delight to my heart, longing
As it does for all that is rare and sublime.
But to enjoy your loveliness I crave
That you might descend where I can reach.
With this thought I content myself:
When your reproving insight my sin so
Reveals, of loving your lowly state, and
Hating it as lofty, to yourself a pardon
You will grant for having been its cause.

XVIII

Lady, you drive death from my thoughts
With great force, impeding my soul
With a grace it might be happier without.
Fruit has fallen and the rind already dry –
Fruit once sweet now bitter to my taste;
So brief are these short hours with you
That I'm tormented by what infinite pleasure
Such a small space offers. In revealing
Such mercy to me, your late, powerful pity
So frightens me, causing death to my body

And torment to my delight. Yet at my age
I thank you: if I die in this state, then your
Mercy will have preserved me from death.

XIX

High lady, to be less unworthy of the gift
Of your immense courtesy, at first
My lowly mind tried wholeheartedly
To reciprocate in kind.

Knowing that my own powers can make
No headway in achieving such a goal,
I ask your forgiveness at my boldness
So that my faults grow constantly wiser.

I see clearly how wrong my belief is
That my fleeting and frail acts can match
Your divine grace raining down on me.

Mind, skill, and memory give way: mortal
As I am I can't repay your heavenly gift,
Not even if I tried a thousand times.

XX

If someone is truly bound to another
By receipt of a great favour, as life from death
What possible repayment might render
The debtor discharged and free?

If this were possible, the continual care
Of an infinite mercy by one who serves
Must be given, even if it cannot be
Where such service has been returned.

To hold your graciousness above my state
I yearn, dear lady, that my ingratitude
Be more apparent than my courtesy,

For if, equally, we were to satisfy one another
You who I love could never be my lord:
There's no place for equals in lordship.

XXI

Weak soul, what rough file tear
sat your hide, and wears it away?
When will time free you from its grasp
Laying aside your dangerous and mortal
Veil, that you may return to where
You once were, pure and happy?
Though I've changed my skin
in these last short years, I can't alter
Old habits, which binds and oppress me
With each passing day, whatever the cost.
My love, I'll not hide from you that in my
Fearful and confused state I envy
Those who are dead, so fearful
is my soul, trembling at its fate.
In my last hours, Lord, allow your
Merciful arms to reach out and remove
Me from myself, make of me
One who is ever pleasing to you.

XXII

Sometimes on my right foot, and then
On my left, I lurch in search of salvation
One to the other. Between vice and virtue
I move, wearied by a trouble heart, as one
Who cannot see heaven whose vista
Is lost from sight along every path.
A blank page to your sanctified ink
I hold out, that your love might show me
How I deceive myself. Your compassion
Might then write the truth for my soul
To slowly become master of itself;

Not succumb to errors in what little life
Remains, that I might live less blindly.
High lady, from you I beg to know
Whether in heaven a humble sinner
Will hold a more modest rank
Than he who is perfectly good.

XXIII

Each passing hour the more I flee
and hate myself, the more, dear lady
Do I surrender to you, in hope
Revivified, my soul less fearful
The closer I am to you. What heaven
Has promised me in your face
And in your beautiful eyes, I aspire to
For they are full of salvation.
From what I see in every other face
I begin to realize most clearly
That eyes without a heart
Possess no power. Lights not seen
Before! And see them I should
No less than I desire to do so,
For to see them but rarely is to
Risk forgetting them entirely.

XXIV

From birth I was granted beauty
To be my vocation's faithful guide;
Mirror and light is it for me
In both the arts. He who thinks
Otherwise is mistaken. My eye
Ascends to those heights where
I sit down to paint and sculpt.

If those of rash and stupid opinion
Drag beauty down to the senses
Though every healthy mind

Is borne by it to heaven, let them
Know that an infirm eye does not
Move from the mortal to the divine
Sphere, but remains forever
Fixed there, where any thought
Of rising without grace is a vain hope.

XXV

If pleasure and familiarity
Begin to dominate the eye
An artist loses all judgment
And becomes fearful; he paints
As beautiful what in his heart
Is inferior, lacking true beauty.
I give you my word, dear lady
Neither pleasure nor familiarity
Have seduced me when, so
Rarely do my eyes meet yours –
Those eyes drawn to where
Desire flies only with difficulty.
One moment was enough
To set me on fire; I have never
Looked upon you other than
As you were at that time.

XXVI

Near or far my eyes can see your face
So beautiful, whenever it appears;
Though only my feet, arms, and hands
Can carry me to where ascend my eyes.

Soul, intellect whole and healthy,
Free and unbounded by your eyes
Ascends to your high beauty; ardor, afire
Gives no such privilege to the body,

Mortal, heavy, lacking wings, it cannot
Follow a tiny angel's flight; sight alone
Can rejoice with pride in so doing.

Ah, what heavenly power as you possess
Let it transform my body into a single eye
That no part of me will not in you rejoice.

XXVII

Great beauty, when it scatters flaming ash
Over a thousand hearts, lays one man low
If he bears it alone – not so, if it is borne
By many who make it easy and light.
Just as fire when confined to a small place
Reduces stone to lime, and so dissolves
In an instant when water is added (as I
Have seen with my own eyes), so do I carry
Within me the fire of a thousand lovers
For a divine woman who has cindered
My heart to the very depths of its parts.
My endless tears dissolve what was
Hard and strong: better to be annihilated
Than to burn without ever dying.

XXVIII

My eyes, be certain that time passes
And the hour approaches when tears
Of sorrow will no longer flow.
May compassion keep them open
While my divine lady continues
To live on earth. If grace should
Unlock heaven, as it does for the blessed
What will I have to gaze upon
When my living sun returns there
And parts from every one of us?

XXIX

Whatever does not come from you
Cannot serve my eyes as a mirror
Where my weary heart might rest.
If it sees beauty that doesn't resemble
You, my lady, then it is dead, mere glass
Chipped of its lining, unable to
Reflect before it any object.
Source of encouragement will it be,
A wonder to anyone who despairs
Of your grace ever touching
His unhappy state. Unless you turn
Your beautiful eyes and brows, and so
Make me blessed, in your compassion,
As old as I am: then know that one born
To misery, grace and good luck allow
To prevail over my harsh destiny, so
That by your heavenly nature will
I have been truly conquered.

XXX

A man in a woman, thus a god
Speaks through her lips: in listening
To her, I'll become one who will
Never again be myself. She it is
Who has removed me from myself,
So that beyond myself I will have
Pity on myself; indeed, so far above
The vanity of desire does her
Sweet face spur me towards
Seeing death in all other beauty.
Oh lady, who urges souls to happier
Days through water and fire, I beg
You, make this happen: that I may
Never again return to my former self.

XXXI

If the divine part of an artist observes
Someone's face and gestures through
A multiple power and gives life to stone,
This isn't the result of mere craft.

It operates in the roughest design, before
A steady hand raises a brush, as the divine
Part experiments on the most interesting
Of ideas, thus arranging perfect figures.

So with me. From birth I was a model
Of little worth; but through you, noble
And virtuous lady, I am made perfect.

If your kindness makes what little I possess
Increase, filing away those rough parts, what
Penitence awaits my fierce ardor, if it is
Nor there to chastise and teach me?

XXXII

To one whose taste is healthy and unspoiled
Great delight is the work of the primary art;
In wax, clay, or stone a likeness of the face
Is fashioned: in its gestures, its entire body
A greater vitality is brought to bear.

If time destroys such a work, or distorts
And dismembers it, that initial beauty
Is forever remembered, and holds
To account the very pleasure now lost.

XXXIII

Not unworthy is a soul looking forward
To eternal life, where it will find rest
And peace when with it grows wealthy
That unique coin heaven mints for us
That nature might spend it down here.

XXXIV

Why is it, dear lady, as experiences shows
A live image in hard, alpine stone lasts
Longer than its maker, who with the years
Finds himself reduced to dust?

Nature is conquered by art when the cause
Bows down and yields to its effect. Proof
Lies in the fine figures I create: confronted
By a work of art, defeated are time and death.

Life, my lady, I surrender in either craft
Whether in paint or in stone, creating
A likeness of either of our faces;

So that a thousand years from now
People will know how beautiful you were
Wretched I, nor was I a fool in loving you.

XXXV

Only in living stone does art
Fashion the face of that woman
Alive on earth as long as time
Insists. My creation, yes! of
Her heavenly presence, who
Is its creation, neither mortal
But divine, and not for my eyes
Only. Yet she will depart, after

Lasting so little time among us.
Yet her noble part lacks good
Fortune, because a rock remains
And death will carry off even she.
Who will avenge her demise?
Nature, or course, as only the work
Of her children lasts here below
Unlike her own work, which time
Carries away amid dust.

XXXVI

When an artist chisels in hard stone
He sometimes renders that person
Like himself. And if I carve a woman's
Face bleak and sad, it is my features
I model because she has made me so;
The stone's harshness resembles her
Because I am simply unable to sculpt
Anything other than my pain-filled face
When she so spurns and despises me.
Through the ages art records beauty;
If her wish is to endure, then let her
Make me forever happy, so that I
Might make her eternally beautiful.

XXXVII

Each time appears my lady's face
Before my heart's eye, whether
Weak or strong, death arranges itself
Between these opposing images, yet
Terrifies me more when it drives
Away that muddled facade.

Greater hope has my soul of attaining
Happiness from this outrage, than of
Finding joy in anything else. Love
Undaunted, resorting to its strongest

Arguments, arms itself in defense
And reasons thus:
>   'Everyone
dies only once, and no one is born
a second time; if, before death
Someone dwells in my heart, what
Happens to him when dies that love?

'The soul is freed by the revival
of that love, and acts as a magnet
to attract an ardor so similar
to itself. Thus the soul, like gold
purified by fire, returns to God.'

XXXVIII

Heavy with years, heaven offers me the keys
Of the lady that I turn so as to enter, like
A plumb-line to the center, seeking repose.
Love fits and turns these keys, opens the heart
Of this lady to all those who are true:
Evil and base desires she forbids me
Drawing me up, tired and worthless as I am
To join the godlike few. From her, graces strange
And sweet and of such power emerge
That whoever dies for her, for himself now lives.

XXXIX

Turning your beautiful eyes upon me
Dear lady, myself I do see in your eyes
As you do, gazing into mine. Your eyes
Reflect me as I am, marked by years
Of suffering, while my eyes reflect you
As shining more than any other star.
Heaven is tempted to grow angry
That my ugliness should be seen
In eyes so beautiful – and you, in my
Ugly eyes, reflecting beauty as well.

What occurs within them is no less
Cruel or sad, while through my eyes
You pass into my heart, as you within
Yours shut me out. This only happens
Whenever your pure virtue is hardened
When confronted by what is inferior:
Love requires use to be equal in youth.

XXXX

Why does inner ardor filled with
Firm faith come so slowly, and not
More often, raising me from the earth
And bearing my heart to where it isn't
By its own power permitted to go?

Each interval between one message
Of your love and the next is granted
To me, because rarity has greater value
The more it is desired, not the reverse.

That interval is night, and day the light:
One freezes my heart, the other love
Enflames, as faith burns with a heaven's fire.

XXXXI

Dear lady, your beautiful face showers forth
A divine beauty, and my delight in that beauty
Though distant, is for me so fleeting, that
All delight in you is inseparable. Too difficult
To ascend is any other path, steep or narrow,
For a pilgrim soul like me. I divide my time
In this way: by day I surrender to your eyes
To you at night my heart, leaving me no time
At all to heaven aspire. At birth my destiny
Binds me to your splendor, preventing me
From becoming enflamed by my own desires
if nothing is there to draw my mind to heaven

Unless by grace or mercy: the heart, lady
Is slow to love what the eye cannot see.

XXXXII

For many years, lady, my heart has carried
An image of your face impressed there
And now that your death approaches, may
Love stamp it on your soul as a special
Privilege, so that the weight of your limbs
Might be released from their earthly prison.

May your soul, storm-tossed or calm
Journey safely in the possession of such
Knowledge, warding off its adversaries
Like the Cross. Heavenward may it return
From where nature borrowed you, there to
Act as an exemplar for angels shining
On high, that for the world's good
They might learn to revive a wise spirit
Once more clothed in flesh, so that
When you're gone to your grave, your
Beautiful face may be ever present to us.

XXXXIII

Heaven leant to us a noble lady in the form
Of her white and pure veil, clothing her beauty
So utterly complete, that we must now recover
By avoiding those many who possessed her
In life, if heaven is not to be badly reimbursed.

In one short breath, an instant! God has gathered
Her body back unto Himself from a world
Unaware of it, and removed it from our eyes.
Though hers may be deceased, her sweet
Graceful and holy writings into oblivion
Cannot be cast. As cruel as mercy can be,
Revealing how heaven had leant to those

Who are ugly what she was, it now claims
It back in death, so that we should also die.

XXXXIV

What a wonder, when close to the fire
I found myself burned and destroyed by it-
Who should now, when it has died down
Be tormented and consumed inside, and so
Little by little to ashes reduced?

Source of my heavy torment, so radiant
Was this place that the very sight of it
Gave me joy, where death and anguish
Were to be but a mere holiday and sport.

Now that heaven has robbed me of the
Splendor of her great flame, which set me
On fire even as it nourished me, I've become
An ember burning still. But buried.

If Love doesn't grant me fresh wood
To rekindle a new flame, then not a single
Spark will be left to me, so rapidly
Into ashes am I turning myself.

Appendix

In a contemporary report we possess a full account of the transit of *David* to Piazza Signorelli in Florence:

On the 14th of May 1504, the marble Giant was taken from the Opera. It came out at 24 o'clock, and they broke the wall above the gateway enough to let it pass. That nights some stones were thrown at the Colossus with intent to harm it. Watch had to be kept at night; and it made its way very slowly, bound as it was upright, suspended in the air with enormous beams and an intricate machinery of ropes. It took four days to reach the Piazza, arriving on the 18th at the hour of 12... The Giant was the work of Michelangelo Buonarroti.[42]

---

42 J.A. Symonds, *The Life of Michelangelo*. London: MacMillan & Co. 1911.

One must try to imagine the effect such a huge statue had on the populace when they awoke to observe it proceeding down their streets at window level. Michelangelo carved his *David* with no other guidance than a small wax model and a few drawings. Yet now it had become a Colossus moving slowly down a street towards Piazza Signorelli.